WATCHMEN

AND

PHILOSOPHY

WATCHMEN
AND
PHILOSOPHY

A RORSCHACH
TEST

Edited by
Mark D. White

WILEY

John Wiley & Sons, Inc.

Published by John Wiley & Sons, Inc., Hoboken, New Jersey
Published simultaneously in Canada

For general information about our other products and services, please contact our Customer Care Department within the United States at (800) 762–2974, outside the United States at (317) 572–3993 or fax (317) 572–4002.

Wiley also publishes its books in a variety of electronic formats. Some content that appears in print may not be available in electronic books. For more information about Wiley products, visit our web site at www.wiley.com.

Library of Congress Cataloging-in-Publication Data:

Watchmen and philosophy : a Rorschach test / edited by Mark D. White.
    p.   cm. —(The Blackwell philosophy and pop culture series)
    Includes index.
    ISBN 978-0-470-39685-8 (pbk.)
    1. Moore, Alan, 1953- Watchmen.   2. Comic books, strips, etc.—Moral and ethical aspects. I. White, Mark D.
    PN6728.W386W38 2009
    741.5'942—dc22
                                            2008045525

Printed in the United States of America

10 9 8 7 6 5 4 3 2 1

CONTENTS

ACKNOWLEDGMENTS

They Left It Entirely
in My Hands

I would like to thank Bill Irwin for his ongoing stewardship on this series; he is as closely involved with every book as a series editor can be, and every book carries his indelible stamp. I thank Eric Nelson and Connie Santisteban at Wiley, not only for their continued editorial and promotional support, but also for their love of *Watchmen* and their undying support of this book. My most emphatic thanks go to the contributors, who brought their unique perspectives on *Watchmen* to this book.

Finally, on behalf of everyone involved with this book, I thank Alan Moore and Dave Gibbons, without whom the world of comics, literature, and popular culture would be sorely lacking.

INTRODUCTION

A Rorschach Test

When I picked up the first issue of *Watchmen* from my comic book store in 1986, I had no idea what I was holding in my hands. (After all, I probably picked up the latest *Booster Gold* in the same trip!) But a few pages in, I had a feeling that something was different, and by the end of the final issue, I knew that comics had changed forever.

In *Watchmen*, Alan Moore and Dave Gibbons gave us a glimpse of what a world with costumed heroes might *actually* look like—and it wasn't pretty. This was not the shiny "world of tomorrow" that was so familiar from the Superman comics. The world of *Watchmen* surpassed even the grim and gritty Gotham City and Hell's Kitchen of Frank Miller's Batman and Daredevil stories. These were not your noble, perfect, shiny heroes, either—Nite Owl could be your Uncle Al, and Rorschach could be the crazy guy down the street who talks to pigeons (and thinks they talk back). Even Dr. Manhattan doesn't seem to know what to do with his nearly limitless power. And the Comedian, a man with no superpowers who is allowed to run amok with the sanction of a very corrupt state, may possibly be the most frightening—and realistic—aspect of *Watchmen*.

Although I can usually find something philosophical to say about any comic (even *Booster Gold*), *Watchmen* is an embarrassment of riches to the comics-obsessed philosopher. The longer you stare at it, the more possibilities you see. From the unique metaphysical nature of Dr. Manhattan to the extreme ethical positions of Ozymandias and Rorschach to Nite Owl's paunch and Silk Spectre's heels, Moore and Gibbons created the richest work of comic fiction the world had ever seen, and which continues to fascinate readers today.

In this book, philosophers delve into these issues and more. How does Dr. Manhattan perceive time? How can we justify Ozymandias's grand plan, and should Rorschach have threatened to expose it? What do the two Silk Spectres, mother and daughter, say about the status of women and the state of feminism? How do we feel about the government's involvement with the Comedian and Dr. Manhattan? And is there anything good—dare we say *virtuous*—about Nite Owl's less-than-ripped torso?

Watchmen and Philosophy is a tribute to Moore and Gibbons's masterpiece, not so much adding to its philosophical depth as highlighting it. Whether you followed *Watchmen* one month at a time in the 1980s (and countless times since) or just discovered the graphic novel last week and can't put it down, you know how engaging and disturbing the story is. So, after you read this book, read *Watchmen* again—if you see something in it you didn't see before (yet was always there), then we've done our job. (Hurm.)

PART ONE

THE POLITICS OF POWER: WHO WATCHES THE WATCHMEN?

THE SUPERMAN EXISTS, AND HE'S AMERICAN: MORALITY IN THE FACE OF ABSOLUTE POWER

Christopher Robichaud

The Son of a Watchmaker

We've all heard the Spider-Man saying "With great power comes great responsibility." But what kind of responsibility comes with *absolute* power? In the world of *Watchmen*, a freak accident turns physicist Jonathan Osterman into Dr. Manhattan, a kind of "superman" who is able to perceive events atemporally, live indefinitely, manipulate matter at its most basic level, and travel unaided to distant worlds. In short, there's very little Dr. Manhattan wants to do that he can't do. And this puts him in a rather unique position. Dr. Manhattan doesn't just have great power, he has a whole different magnitude of power, a kind of hyper-power that makes him, in the estimation of the esteemed Professor Milton Glass, more or less a god on Earth.[1] God's American, too—and that's not a trivial fact. Dr. Manhattan's status as a U.S. "asset" gives the America of *Watchmen* an even greater technological and military advantage than it has in actuality.

But the existence of such a superpowerful and superintelligent being who lives among mere mortals—at least for a time—invites us to consider several questions that fall within the purview of moral philosophy. Is Dr. Manhattan any longer capable of reasoning about right and wrong in the way that he did as Jonathan Osterman? What force does morality really have over someone as powerful as him? And how ought the United States itself behave, given the supreme international dominance it has in virtue of Dr. Manhattan's existence?

Rubble and the Human Race

Let's begin by looking more closely at Dr. Manhattan's thoughts and actions. A little way into *Watchmen*, he leaves Earth to reside on Mars. His departure is spurred by public accusations that his presence causes those close to him to develop cancer. (This turns out to be false; the rumor was spread by Ozymandias as part of his plan to eliminate, one way or the other, the heroes who would stand in the way of his grand scheme.) But Dr. Manhattan had withdrawn emotionally from the world long before his physical departure, as his partner Laurie Juspeczyk, the second Silk Spectre, would readily acknowledge. As a result, Dr. Manhattan no longer finds much value in the human race; in particular, he finds it difficult to care about the pressing problem immediately confronting it, that of possibly having to endure a nuclear war, the threat of which is, in part, due to his decision to take up residency on Mars.

What exactly is going on with Dr. Manhattan? We've just made three important claims. The first is that he's having difficulty finding human beings morally valuable. The second is that he's somehow emotionally absent. And the third is that this absence is the cause of his, let us say, moral ambivalence. Can we defend these assertions?

The first is the least controversial; in fact, it's supported outright when Laurie presses her case for Dr. Manhattan to return to Earth: "I mean, ordinary people . . . All the things that happen to them . . . Doesn't that move you more than a bunch of rubble?" Dr. Manhattan replies, "No. I read atoms, Laurie. I see the ancient spectacle that birthed the rubble. Beside this, human life is brief and mundane."[2] This makes it pretty clear that Dr. Manhattan doesn't see human beings as possessing the kind of moral value we think they do. But why doesn't he?

My suggestion is that Dr. Manhattan's attitude toward humans is best explained by his lack of some kind of crucial emotional capacity. This idea can be resisted, however. For one thing, we might think that his moral attitude toward humans is simply the result of his supreme intelligence and power, without having anything specific to do with his emotions. That doesn't seem plausible, though. Concerning his intelligence, it's true that Dr. Manhattan is able to experience the natural world in a fundamentally different way from how human beings do—he can "read atoms," after all—but the world he's in contact with is not a mysterious one that ordinary physicists aren't aware of. Stephen Hawking is well versed in the scope of the cosmos and our tiny place in it, yet he doesn't consider humans to be morally on a par with rubble. And concerning Dr. Manhattan's power, we humans have power over young children comparable to what he has over us. And yet we don't think this makes children morally insignificant. So the explanation of Dr. Manhattan's moral ambivalence can't rest solely on the nature of his intelligence or abilities.

A different way to resist our explanatory claim is to point out, rightly, that Dr. Manhattan does experience some emotions; he gets angry during the television interview when he's falsely accused of being carcinogenic, and he also seems to feel jealousy over Laurie's budding relationship with Dan Dreiberg, the second Nite Owl. But using the work of philosopher Jesse Prinz, especially as presented in his book *The*

Emotional Construction of Morals, we can distinguish moral from nonmoral emotions.[3] According to Prinz, moral emotions, like indignation, are "built up" out of nonmoral ones, like anger. It's important to note, however, that moral emotions aren't identical to nonmoral ones—they're unique.

So we can revise our original idea by claiming that while Dr. Manhattan might possess nonmoral emotions, he lacks moral ones. And this absence isn't merely a kind of withdrawal. It's not that Dr. Manhattan is simply depressed. Rather, it seems plausible that the atomic accident that led to his disintegration and subsequent reintegration, while granting him powers almost beyond our imagination, nevertheless robbed him of the capacity to experience moral emotions.

Emotions: They're Not Just for Breakfast Anymore

But so what? Even if we grant that Dr. Manhattan lacks the capacity to experience these kinds of emotions, how does that explain his inability to value persons properly? In other words, what role do such emotions play in moral reasoning? The answer, according to many philosophers, starting with David Hume (1711–1776), is: quite a lot![4] Unfortunately, agreement ends there. *Emotivists*, who see themselves as following in the tradition of Hume, think that moral reasoning (if it even is reasoning) simply amounts to the possession and expression of emotions. So when we say, "What Ozymandias does at the end of *Watchmen* is wrong," all we're doing is expressing a negative moral emotion—such as indignation—toward his action.

Others think, more plausibly, that moral reasoning has more substance than that; in particular, they think that when we say, "What Ozymandias does at the end of *Watchmen* is wrong," we're expressing the *thought* that what he does is wrong, which isn't just the expression of an emotion. But emotions play an important role in forming such thoughts. Again turning to an idea motivated by Prinz, we can say that we need moral emotions to possess the *concepts* of moral rightness, wrongness, goodness, and badness.[5] So if Dr. Manhattan lacks moral emotions, he no longer possesses the things needed to properly form beliefs about what's morally right and wrong. And this explains his inability to judge humans as having the value we all believe them as having.

It's worth asking, though, why we should accept the idea that emotions play this central role in moral thinking. Consider Immanuel Kant (1724–1804), who claimed that the morally right actions are those that conform to the categorical imperative—they're the actions that treat people as ends in themselves and not merely as means.[6] Although it would take some work, we can determine whether, say, Rorschach's act of dispensing with Big Figure conforms to the categorical imperative (want to take a guess whether it does?). We can also thereby judge his action as being morally right or wrong without reference to any moral emotions whatsoever. So while we may not *in fact* lack the relevant emotions needed, because of the way we're hard-wired, it's nevertheless *possible* for us to lack these emotions and yet make moral judgments.

We can challenge this possibility, however. To borrow a gruesome but effective example from Gilbert Harman, imagine that we stumbled upon some people pouring gasoline over a cat, preparing to set it on fire.[7] No doubt, we would judge this action to be wrong. But suppose also that one of us, call her Alice, simply doesn't *feel* anything at all upon witnessing the event. No moral outrage, no moral disgust, nothing. Let's assume she still says the same thing we do: "That's wrong!" Even so, it seems reasonable to conclude that Alice is merely parroting our words. She hasn't *really* formed and expressed the thought that burning the cat alive is wrong—how could she have, if she feels *nothing*.

Similarly, if Alice appears to judge that the right thing to do is to try to stop these villains but feels absolutely no compulsion to do so, that, too, would suggest that she really doesn't believe that it's the right thing to do. And this is because there's good reason to suppose that moral beliefs are intrinsically motivating; when we form a belief that something is right or wrong, doing so *by itself* motivates us to action. If emotions are part of that process, then the motivational aspect of forming moral beliefs is easy to appreciate, since emotions often do motivate us to action.

Admittedly, these thoughts do not amount to a knock-down argument against the possibility that persons without emotions can nevertheless hold robust thoughts about what is morally right and wrong and good and bad. But it should make us suspicious that this *apparent* possibility is in fact a genuine one. We'll continue, then, with the analysis we've been suggesting about what's wrong with Dr. Manhattan. He lacks the emotions necessary to form appropriate moral judgments, and this explains his ambivalence toward the value of persons. Sadly, this is not a very uplifting prognosis of his condition, for it suggests that even though Dr. Manhattan has superhuman power and intelligence, he can't do something important that Joe and Jane Ordinary can: he can't reason properly about what's right and wrong. This is a particularly troubling fact, given just how much power Dr. Manhattan has at his disposal; indeed, given his ambitions at the end of *Watchmen* to create human life somewhere in the universe, it's a downright frightening fact. The idea of a morally ambivalent god is not comforting.

Sure, It's the Right Thing to Do—Now Tell Me Why I Should Do It

Whether Dr. Manhattan is himself capable of adequately thinking about right and wrong, it's nevertheless reasonable to think that he's subject to the very same moral mandates, permissions, and restrictions that the rest of us are subject to. Put succinctly, Dr. Manhattan has an obligation to do the right thing and to avoid doing the wrong thing. So if, returning to Kant for a moment, it's true that we have an obligation to act in ways that treat people as ends and not merely as means, then Dr. Manhattan has that obligation, too. And if we therefore wouldn't have been permitted to kill Rorschach at the end of *Watchmen* just because we disagreed with his decision to expose Ozymandias, then Dr. Manhattan wasn't permitted to do so, either. His supreme intelligence and power—his god-like standing—do not exempt him from being held to the same moral standards that the rest of us are held to, whatever those might end up being.

This is a compelling line of thought, summed up nicely by the slogan that no one is above the moral law. But it invites a further question. Why, exactly, is no one above it? Even by philosophical standards, this is a deep question. It is asking, in essence, what the *grounds* of morality are—what gives moral principles their force over us? And it's particularly important to consider this question as it concerns Dr. Manhattan, since we ourselves have no way of enforcing moral obligations on him should he choose not to follow them. How does one punish or reward someone who is able to create worlds and simply think people into nonexistence?

We can therefore imagine Dr. Manhattan asking, "Given my intelligence and power, why should I do what morality demands?" One answer that some might find appealing is to say that morality gets its force from God. This *divine command theory* of ethics, as it is often called, claims both that God "bestows" actions with moral properties such as rightness and wrongness and that what compels us to act morally—what gives us an obligation to do the right thing and to avoid doing the wrong thing—is the fact that God wills it.

This response grounds the demands of morality on the existence of God, but even for believers, it isn't a very good way to go. Dr. Manhattan seems pretty skeptical about the existence of God, saying that "existence is random, has no pattern" and referring to the universe as "a clock without a craftsman." So the divine command theorist would have to convince Dr. Manhattan that God exists before providing him with a reason to take the moral law seriously. And given the notorious difficulties with "proving" the existence of God, this approach isn't strategically smart. Moreover, it's unclear exactly why God's willing that certain actions are right or wrong should hold any sway over what Dr. Manhattan does. He might rightfully ask what it is about God that gives God's will this importance in his life. Perhaps it's the threat of God's wrath. But that threat loses much of its force when it's directed against a being as powerful as Dr. Manhattan is. Maybe instead it's the *nature* of God that gives God's will its binding force. But the all-knowing, all-powerful nature of God is something Dr. Manhattan more or less shares, so he might understandably wonder why his own will isn't as effective as God's in this matter.

Kant offers a different approach. For him, all rational creatures are subject to acting in accordance with the categorical imperative, and that's because the demand of morality is a rational one; it is, according to Kant, *irrational* not to act morally. The irrationality doesn't so much have to do with acting against one's self-interest, but in willing or affirming contradictions. What does that mean? The details are unfortunately quite thorny. Happily, we needn't concern ourselves with them, but unhappily, that's because it doesn't seem likely that Kant's approach will work in the case of Dr. Manhattan. And that's because, however the specific story goes about why acting morally amounts to acting rationally, it assumes that morality only binds *rational* agents. And it's not clear that Dr. Manhattan is rational!

Here's why. No one's questioning the intellect of Dr. Manhattan. But for him to count as fully rational in the sense that will give morality rational sway over him, he needs to possess the conceptual apparatus necessary for forming moral thoughts. This is why, in Kant's view, nonhuman animals aren't subject to the moral law; while they can certainly reason about certain things, they aren't fully rational, because they lack certain conceptual capabilities. Now Kant thinks that one doesn't need moral emotions to be able to form moral thoughts, but we disagree and have previously provided reasons supporting our position. If that's right, however, then Dr. Manhattan shares the same lot that nonhuman animals do when it comes to the moral law. He isn't subject to it, because he isn't fully rational.

So maybe Dr. Manhattan is above (or below?) the moral law. But that would seem to be due to a technicality. It's one thing to think that bears aren't subject to moral evaluation when they attack people who unwittingly trespass on their turf; it's quite another to think that someone as intelligent and as sophisticated as Dr. Manhattan is likewise unbound by moral demands. Perhaps, then, the best answer to his question as to why he ought to do what the moral law requires is a resounding "Because!" Obviously, that sounds rather unsatisfying (just ask a child). But everyone agrees that analysis stops somewhere. Maybe it's just a brute fact, admitting of no further explanation, that beings like Dr. Manhattan ought to do the right thing and avoid doing the wrong thing, period. This means that we were on the wrong track in assuming that there needed to be a substantive answer to Dr. Manhattan's question. Even philosophers should sometimes let certain questions lie.

From the Personal to the Political

Let's proceed, then, by assuming that Dr. Manhattan has the same moral responsibilities that the rest of us do. Our last question is what responsibilities the United States has in light of the fact that Dr. Manhattan has signed on as an official military asset. This is a question of political morality, and it concerns the moral mandates, permissions, and restrictions that states have toward one another. Specifically, we want to know whether the United States, given the huge strategic advantage it has with Dr. Manhattan in its employ, is morally permitted to adopt a "double-standard" when it comes to its international behavior, insisting that other nations behave in ways that it doesn't.

It might seem that we've already answered this question. If Dr. Manhattan himself isn't above the moral law in virtue of his power and intellect, it seems only reasonable to conclude that the United States isn't above the moral law in virtue of the power it inherits from his service. That certainly should be our default position, but it's important to point out that political morality is different from personal morality. Nations aren't persons, and so it's not necessarily inconsistent to claim that while Dr. Manhattan has to play by the same moral rules that every other person has to play by, the United States as a country does not have to play by the same moral rules that other countries have to. Just because we've taken a stand on a question involving personal morality doesn't mean we are thereby committed to taking the same stand on a question involving political morality.

It's also important to keep in mind that we're not primarily concerned with what it's permissible for Dr. Manhattan himself to do, acting alone, when it comes to international affairs. Since he's employed by the U.S. government, he has subjected his will to its will when acting in a military capacity. So our question, again, is what it's permissible for the United States to do, given the hyper-power it's become due to Dr. Manhattan's service. We are not concerned with whether Dr. Manhattan ought to involve himself personally in international affairs, beyond the legitimate mandate he receives by acting as an agent of the United States.

Having said that, why in the world should we think that the United States is morally permitted to do things others nations aren't, like, say, engaging in preventive wars and advancing protectionist economic policies? David Luban, although an opponent of the double-standard view of American policy, has examined some of the arguments that have been mustered in its defense.[8] He first points out that if the idea is going to be plausible at all, it best not be justified along the lines of, "The United States is permitted to do it because it can get away with it." If that's the whole story, that's no story at all. But there are more compelling reasons to think that a hyper-power is permitted to act on the international stage in ways other countries aren't.

One line of reasoning Luban looks at claims that the best way of promoting the emergence of more democracies, of advancing more economic stability, and of securing more meaningful freedoms—all very good things, no doubt—is for the United States to act in its own self-interest, involving itself in the affairs of other nations in a way that is impermissible for other nations to do. Another line of reasoning explored by Luban claims that the United States is granted permissions other nations don't have because it endures costs that other nations don't. By acting as the "sheriff," it makes itself more of a target and puts U.S. soldiers and resources on the line. The idea is that the more it is willing to risk losing, the more costs it is willing to take on, the more permissions it gains.

Neither of these arguments are very compelling, though. Luban rightly points out that the first one rests heavily on a dubious assumption, namely, that every time the United States acts in a self-beneficial way on the world stage, it also somehow promotes good things beyond its borders. Sometimes this is undoubtedly true, but surely not always. And even if it were always true, the reasoning involved faces a more fundamental flaw when the role of Dr. Manhattan's service to his country is taken into account. Given his more or less absolute power, and given that it would be in America's best interest to deal with a world where all countries are peaceful, freedom-loving democracies, it seems permissible according to this view for the United States to launch a world war to attain this goal. With Dr. Manhattan's powers, there's little doubt that the United States would win, probably at very little cost to itself. And it would be acting both in its interests and in the interests of the other nations and people of the world; when the dust settled, many persons would be living under better conditions than they now live under. Still, it is deeply counter-intuitive to think that these facts morally warrant the United States in waging such a war, with Dr. Manhattan leading the charge. That's because we think that nations have a certain right to sovereignty—a right to self-determination—that they don't forfeit unless they start committing heinous acts within themselves or start waging war with other nations.

The second line of reasoning is equally problematic in light of Dr. Manhattan's service to his country. Given his powers, the United States really doesn't take on any additional risks by acting as the world's sheriff. There's little that can be thrown at the United States that Dr. Manhattan can't stop or undo. So if the risks need to be genuine to warrant lopsided permissions, the United States doesn't satisfy this condition. In the absence of further arguments in favor of U.S. "exceptionalism," then, it seems that even though Dr. Manhattan makes it a hyper-power with absolutely no serious rivals on the international stage, the United States must nevertheless behave as all other nations do.

The Endless Ethical Enigmas of Dr. Manhattan (There Oughta Be a Book . . .)

We've looked at a variety of moral issues surrounding the existence of Dr. Manhattan, a unique and powerful entity in the *Watchmen* universe. And there are plenty more questions to consider. Is it morally appropriate for him to leave Earth after the devastating attack by Ozymandias? Can any plausible defense be given of his choice to kill Rorschach? Would it be permissible for him to create human life elsewhere in the cosmos? These are all worthwhile things to ponder, but it is perhaps worth noting that Dr. Manhattan already knows how we'll answer them, when we'll do so, where we'll be, and what he thinks about them. And that is either a very comforting or a very terrifying thought.

NOTES

1. *Watchmen*, chap. IV, supplemental material, excerpt from *Dr. Manhattan: Super-Powers and the Superpowers*, by Professor Milton Glass, p. ii.

2. Ibid., chap. IX, pp. 16–17.

3. Oxford, UK: Oxford University Press, 2007.

4. See Hume's *A Treatise on Human Nature*, ed. David and Mary Norton (Oxford, UK: Oxford University Press, 2000).

5. Prinz, *The Emotional Construction of Morals* (Oxford, UK: Oxford University Press, 2007), chap. 1.

6. See Kant's *Groundwork of the Metaphysics of Morals*, ed. Mary Gregor (Cambridge, UK: Cambridge University Press, 1997).

7. See Harman's *The Nature of Morality: An Introduction to Ethics* (New York: Oxford University Press, 1977), chap. 1.

8. "Preventive War," *Philosophy and Public Affairs* (July 2004): 207–248.

CAN WE STEER THIS RUDDERLESS WORLD? KANT, RORSCHACH, RETRIBUTIVISM, AND HONOR

Jacob M. Held

> Because there is good and evil, and evil must be
> punished. Even in the face of Armageddon I shall not
> compromise this. But there are so many deserving of
> retribution . . . and there is so little time.
>
> —Rorschach's journal, October 13, 1985. 11:30 P.M.

Rorschach carries a terrific burden. He has seen the true face of the city. He has seen this world full of vermin for what it is: a cesspool of the wretched, each climbing over the back of his or her neighbor for nothing but one more trifling pleasure, to simply continue this pathetic life for one second, one minute, or one day longer. So, what do you do when confronted with such filth? Do you walk by and pretend there is no infestation? Do you focus only on the least repulsive and delude yourself into the belief that the world is good underneath it all? Or do you become an exterminator, stomping all the human cockroaches you can while relentlessly pursuing the rest? You'll never get them all, for they scurry to the shadows when the light is turned on. But you can get some; you can make a difference. And even if all you manage is a tiny ripple in the fetid slime, at least you lived respectably; you never became one.

The mind of Rorschach is indeed a dark place, yet it's ruled by a simple principle with a long and venerable heritage: evil must be punished. And it must be punished not because doing so makes the world a better place, but simply because it is evil and thus is deserving of punishment. Rorschach thus exemplifies the *retributive theory of punishment*. He maintains that wrongdoers must be punished for no other reason than that they did wrong; they deserve it. Likewise, the punishment they receive must be fitting. You don't execute a petty thief and, some might argue, you don't let murderers live or, for Rorschach at least, even multiple rapists. A retributivist dishes out just desert; you get what you deserve, and what you deserve is dictated by the heinousness of your deeds.

To some degree, we all desire retribution. We are all a little bit Rorschach. We all want to see wrongs righted and wicked people suffering. There is no shame in this, even if retribution often looks shameful. Rorschach, as is befitting his name, lets us see ourselves. Through him, we see our desire for justice pushed to its limits. With him, we see an uncompromising goal of meting out just deserts, its beauty and its horror. After witnessing Rorschach's torturous ways and his lack of respect for any sense of rights, all in his quest to give people what they deserve, and even after we celebrate when he dispatches a murderous kidnapper in an oddly satisfactory way, we should ask a few questions: Why *must* evil be punished? Who determines what evil is? Who determines what is appropriate, or fitting, punishment? And in our quest to dispense deserved justice, do we risk becoming the monsters against which we battle?[1]

You don't have to think too hard to see the connection between Rorschach and the Black Freighter, as our castaway feeds on "raw shark," becoming darker and more sinister with every bite, in his quest to give what is owed to the demon ship.[2] He himself becomes a demon. His mission is no longer about his love for his family and his desire to protect them but merely about wreaking vengeance on the demon ship; revenge pure and simple, blood lust. We should look at Rorschach and ask, Is it all about vengeance or is there something nobler in retribution or in paying back a criminal for his crime? In what follows, we'll give retributivism a Rorschach test to see whether what lies beneath the mask is attractive or just fascinatingly ugly.[3]

Evil Must Be Punished: Retributivism, Basically

The city is dying of rabies. Is the best I can do to wipe random flecks of foam from its lips? Never despair. Never surrender.

—Rorschach's journal, October 13, 1985

What compels Rorschach? If it were mere vengeance, a thirst for revenge, or simple hatred, he would be a much less interesting character. If all he wanted to do was hurt people out of sadistic urges and cover it over with the name of justice, reminiscent of Hooded Justice, he would be easy to ignore or condemn. But there is so much more to Rorschach. His motives are pure; it is about justice, right, and the moral order. In this way, he reflects what is desirable about retributivism: the guilty must be punished because they are guilty, and their punishment should be proportionate to their crimes. This sentiment is common, even if its justification is difficult to articulate.

Retributivism comes in many different varieties, but most basic formulations seem to include three elements: (1) only the guilty are to be punished, that is, you punish someone only for a voluntary wrongdoing; (2) the punishment must be equivalent to the wickedness done; and 3) the justification for punishing persons is that the return of suffering for wrong doing is itself morally good.[4] The idea is that if someone causes harm or inflicts suffering on another, this warrants punishment—and the punishment ought to fit the severity of the wrongdoer's misdeeds. Some argue that there is no deeper justification for retributivism, that it's impossible to prove but nonetheless true. It's simply just to return like for like; paying wrongdoers back is both justified *and* good. But, as we'll see, there is a more elaborate justification, tied to respect, honor, and what it means to be a valuable person living a worthwhile life in a community of other moral persons.

When Rorschach administers punishment, say by drowning Big Figure in the toilet, even if at this point he is a very small threat indeed, he is administering the ancient law of retaliation, or *lex talionis* ("an eye for an eye"). Big Figure is surely a murderer (and probably worse), so in order for justice to be done, he must receive his payment in full. As we would expect, then, before Rorschach flees, he complies with the demands of justice and dispenses quick, wet justice to Big Figure.[5] But the idea that we should harm another person simply because that person caused harm is often seen as brutal, barbarous, and a relic of the past. Indeed, drowning a midget in a toilet isn't aesthetically pleasing; it doesn't look "right."

Thus, some people argue that the notion of an eye for an eye ought to be done away with and replaced with a more humane principle, such as rehabilitation or concern for the greater good. But to characterize retribution as simply returning harm for harm, as if it were rationalized revenge, is simplistic at best, disingenuous and misleading at worst. Even though in its most simplistic and extreme formulations, the *lex talionis* may lead to questionable practices such as killing a multiple rapist without a trial, that does not mean the principle is flawed.[6] Rorschach may simply be an overly enthusiastic (and not too reflective) practitioner of an otherwise praiseworthy practice. We can disagree with Rorschach's distribution of punishment without having to condemn the practice. Perhaps we ought to give criminals what they deserve, and Rorschach is just not that good at determining or dispensing just deserts.

Retributivism is clearly not a *consequentialist* idea—it is not an idea justified by its results. Under retributivism, we don't punish criminals and wrongdoers because the punishment lowers crime rates, leads to rehabilitation, provides security, is cost effective, makes us feel good, or leads to any other desirable result. We punish those who deserve it because they deserve it, period. On this, there can be no compromise. Rorschach is unbending in his commitment to justice, just as was his philosophical progenitor, Immanuel Kant (1724–1804). Since Kant gives us the modern formulation of the *lex talionis*, it is to Kant whom we now turn.

Kant and Rorschach on Respect and Dignity

> We do not do this because it is permitted. We do it because we have to. We do it because we are compelled.
>
> —Rorschach (from the notes of Dr. Malcolm Long, October 27, 1985)

Kant stated simply enough, "[Punishment] must always be inflicted upon [the criminal] only *because he has committed a crime*."[7] Punishment shouldn't be meted out for the criminal's own good, for example, for reformation or rehabilitation. This would be treating him like an animal, like a dog. Also, punishment shouldn't be handed out for the good of society, such as for security, deterrence, or crime prevention or any other desirable end. The criminal shouldn't be treated as a mere means; we shouldn't *use* people for society's ends, "for a human being can never be treated merely as a means to the purposes of another."[8] By this, Kant meant that people deserve respect. But why respect criminals? Didn't they lose this right? To understand why criminals must be punished because of what they did, and why their punishment must respect them as moral agents—that is, as wrongdoers to be held accountable for their actions—we need to look briefly at Kant's ethics.

The aspects of Kant's moral system we are most interested in are best illustrated by one of the versions of his famous *categorical imperative*: "So act that you use humanity, whether in your own person or in the person of any other, always at the same time as an end, never merely as a means."[9] Herein lay two fundamental concepts for Kant: dignity and respect. All human beings insofar as they are *autonomous*—that is, can be the author of their own actions and determine the principles on which they will act—possess inherent dignity. They can decide to act on those principles, or maxims, that correspond with the "moral law" as described by the categorical imperative, or they can act out of selfish desires and self-interest and hence act immorally. Each person's capacity to make this choice proves his or her moral value or dignity, and by virtue of this dignity, persons deserve respect, to be treated always as valuable ends in themselves and never only as means to someone else's ends.

So basically, our status as dignified, moral agents obligates others to respect us and limits how they may treat us. And yes, criminals are people, too. Furthermore, in order to treat the criminal as a human being with dignity, we can punish him only if he has committed a crime. To punish him merely to send a signal to others, or for any other consequentialistic or utilitarian reason, is to use him merely as a means, and this is unacceptable, regardless of whom we are punishing. As Kant said, "The law of punishment is a categorical imperative, and woe to him who crawls through the windings of eudaemonism in order to discover something that releases the criminal from punishment or even reduces its amount by the advantage it promises . . . for justice ceases to be justice if it can be bought for any price whatsoever."[10] But if we don't punish criminals for their own good, for society's benefit, or because it makes us feel better, then why do we do it? Why *must* we punish the guilty?

Order and Value in a Morally Blank World

> The void breathed hard on my heart, turning its
> illusions to ice, shattering them. Was reborn then,
> free to scrawl own design on this morally blank world.
>
> —Rorschach (from the notes of Dr. Malcolm Long,
> October 28, 1985)

What if society was founded on a set of values such as dignity and respect? These fundamental values would give human endeavors and human life their meaning, and maintaining them would be essential. In such a world, punishment would be—perhaps paradoxically—a reaffirmation of these values, mending the social fabric that was torn asunder by criminal wrongdoing.

Consider a trivial Rorschach example: his chastisement of Moloch for owning illegal prescription drugs and an unregistered firearm. We might ask, "Why do you care? He isn't hurting anybody, right?" By breaking the law, Moloch is flaunting social norms, rules that hold the fabric of society together. In possessing drugs and a gun illegally, Moloch is making a statement that he does not share our common values or respect us enough to play by the rules. Rorschach's world is ordered by common values, and deviants threaten its cohesiveness. But even if we don't live in such a world, one could argue that we ought to strive for it; perhaps our dignity is found in acting as if the world were just, even when it clearly is not.

In general, we punish the criminal because it is demanded that he be held accountable for wrongdoing, and to do otherwise is disrespectful to him. If we failed to punish him, we would not be treating him as a full member of the moral community. We also punish the criminal in order to mend the social fabric and reaffirm the values he disregarded, including the value of the victim and his or her loss in cases of crimes against a person. As G. W. F. Hegel (1770–1831) noted, "[Punishment] is the cancellation of crime . . . and the restoration of right."[11] We can't literally make a victim or society whole in the sense of restoring them to the state they were in before the crime occurred, but through punishment we can reaffirm the values that were transgressed and make the criminal *feel* the wrong he committed. This is the true sense of retribution, "to pay back," to even the scales put askew by an act of criminal wrongdoing. We must punish because we value one another and society, because we respect the inherent dignity in each of us and wish to reaffirm these values on which our lives and society are, or ought to be, based. Punishment is one way we reproduce what makes life worth living—it is a tribute to life.

Arguably, then, punishment is meant to protect and reproduce an ideal moral order. Each person is to respect others and treat them as ends in themselves, that is, as people deserving of respect in virtue of what they are: free, rational agents. Punishment is merely an instrument for implementing this moral order. As Rorschach so poetically put it, "This rudderless world is not shaped by vague metaphysical forces. It is not god who kills the children. Not fate that butchers them or destiny that feeds them to the dogs. It's us. Only us."[12] Values are not to be found in nature; the world isn't good in itself, but rather it is made so through our actions. Life's value is in how it is lived. Kant stated, "For if justice goes, there is no longer any value in human beings' living on the earth."[13] Without an order of right, without justice and ethical human relations, there is nothing but brute animals, human cockroaches left to their heroin and child pornography. But with justice and ethics, there comes value and respect. Thus, how we punish expresses society's values.[14] Do we punish because it benefits us? Do we use people? Or do we punish because they have done wrong and deserve it? Do we punish because moral agents need to be held accountable, and society's fundamental values need to be reestablished and maintained?

Giving some persons their just deserts is holding them accountable to public values that ideally respect their worth as persons with dignity, even if they experience and act upon a moral lapse.[15] And to answer your question, Laurie: Yes, rape is a moral lapse—one of the most grave, to be sure, but it in no way removes one from the community of moral agents. When we punish, we retain our connection to the criminal and his bond to the moral community. He is held to the values that define and give value to our shared human lives. There is much more than revenge or vengeance going on behind the mask of retributivism. One might even say that at root, it is a matter of honor.[16]

Honor Is Like the Hawk . . .

> For my own part, regret nothing. Have lived life, free from compromise . . . and step into the shadow now without complaint.
>
> —Rorschach's journal, November 1, 1985

According to Kant, "Rightful honor consists in asserting one's worth as a human being in relation to others."[17] So we ought to treat one another as free, moral agents; we ought to respect one another. If I deceive you, use you, or otherwise manipulate you, then I disparage your life and my own. It should be clear that Rorschach operates under this code. He is consistent, honest, transparent, and, above all else, honorable in his treatment of others. They are treated as their actions merit; they are respected as the authors of their acts.

At the very end of *Watchmen*, Rorschach stands outside Veidt's complex staring down the barrel of a loaded
Dr. Manhattan. He is going back. Evil must be punished.
People must be told. If he lets Veidt get away with his scheme,
then justice has been bought, not served. And, as Kant noted,
without justice there is no value in human life. Without our
dignity as moral agents, and without our self-respect and
our honor, we are shameful. Regardless of the price, if you sell
your dignity you're a whore, and while Rorschach may be a
whore's son, he's no whore. Rorschach refuses to compromise,
to sell out justice, even if it means dispelling the illusion Veidt
created and thereby guaranteeing that the millions who died
did so in vain. As tears stream down, knowing his fate, he yells
at Dr. Manhattan, "Do it!" and Dr. Manhattan evaporates
him. Rorschach did not seek death; he didn't commit suicide
by Manhattan. But he understood what the others did not.
"It is better to sacrifice life than to forfeit morality. It is not
necessary to live, but it is necessary that, so long as we live, we
do so honourably."[18] Even in the face of Armageddon, never
compromise. Life is not valuable simply in virtue of not
being death.

The absolute value of one's life, one's inherent dignity,
stems from autonomy or freedom, the ability to act according
to the moral law. Life isn't valuable; freedom is.[19] So it is that an
honorable man is one who acknowledges this and lives a life of
duty and not one subservient to the trivial pleasures of animal
existence. No regrets, no compromise. "[An upright man] lives
only from duty, not because he has the least taste for living."[20]
Thus rightful or true honor is the manifestation of one's life as
a moral agent, and society reflects the praiseworthiness of the
moral, upright life by publicly affirming the value of honor and
shaming those who have acted dishonorably—that is, immorally
or criminally. Punishment, as a public statement, is a shaming,
a dishonoring of the wrongdoer that is meant to reinforce social
values, attribute blameworthiness to the wrongdoer, and so

reintegrate that person into the moral order. We punish only those we dignify as moral agents, and we punish them because we respect them.

This Last Entry

Gradually, I understood what innocent intent had brought me to, and, understanding, waded out beyond my depth.

—"The Black Freighter," *Watchmen*, chapter XI, p. 13

So Rorschach exemplifies the retributive spirit, giving back to each his rightful due, out of respect for him as a person and respect for those values he has denigrated through his wrongdoing. Payback is about more than returning harm for harm; it is about balancing the scales, restoring order, and affirming fundamental values. Punishment is a social practice legitimated as supportive of the social fabric that gives us meaning, that is, the moral context by which we judge ourselves and others and discern moral praiseworthiness. But people do object to this notion. And Rorschach is not without his flaws. We probably wouldn't want to live in a world of his making. Why?

Most objections to retributivism don't attack the idea of respect or dignity. Rather, they see the problem as one of application. How do we determine someone's just desert? Who determines a fitting punishment? Who determines which values are essential, how they ought to be affirmed, and so on? And to be sure, Rorschach is brutal. He kills those whom he claims deserve it. But should he alone determine desert? Perhaps the main objection people have against retributivism is not whether people deserve anything or even whether it can be calculated. Most people probably object because there needs to be a check on the practice so that it doesn't get out of hand. We don't want to go from Rorschach to "raw shark."

We probably don't even want to go as far as Rorschach. We may doubt the certainty of our moral knowledge without doubting its necessity. We live in a nonideal world, but that doesn't mean we need to live without ideals.

Perhaps all that we require is a simple check, something to balance our moral judgments. Such a check might merely be dialogue. Often an open discourse, an understanding of our history and our prospective future, can shed light on our present, put it in perspective and so serve a humbling function, freeing us from the hubris of our intellectual arrogance—when we assume that we know what is right or wrong, that we know what people deserve and couldn't possibly be wrong. Rorschach's shortcoming is that he never listened to anyone; he was overly confident and proud. When they disagreed with him, he called them decadent; when they wanted to bargain, he called it compromise—and for him there was no more disgraceful a word. Rorschach was judge, jury, and executioner, or, more accurately, the legislative, executive, and judicial branches all in one. And although each branch may be essential for justice, they function justly only when they function as independent checks on the others. The problem with retributivism isn't the idea; it's the application. If Rorschach had just a little humility, had recognized he might be wrong and others might be right, he might not be so fascinatingly *ugly*.[21]

NOTES

1. Chapter VI of *Watchmen* ends with a famous quote by Nietzsche, "Battle not with monsters, lest ye become a monster." See Friedrich Nietzsche, *Beyond Good and Evil: Prelude to a Philosophy of the Future*, ed. Rolf-Peter Horstmann, trans. Judith Norman (Cambridge, UK: Cambridge University Press, 2002), p. 69.

2. The "raw shark"/Rorschach connection is clearly made in *Watchmen*, chap. V, p. 22.

3. I had to make a bad Rorschach pun. I apologize to the reader. It's out of my system now.

4. See H. L. A. Hart, *Punishment and Responsibility: Essays in the Philosophy of Law* (New York: Oxford University Press, 1968), pp. 230–237.

5. Of course, Rorschach is acting here as a vigilante and not as a functionary of the penal system, and the distinction is important. But for the remainder of this essay, we can deal

with Rorschach and his version of retribution as if he were a legitimate state authority who could mete out punishment. Vigilantism is another issue entirely.

6. Again, the question is about determining fitting punishments and not whether vigilantism is justified. Beyond the obvious problem of Rorschach's executing criminals without trial, we may still wish to ask whether execution is a fitting punishment for rape, and for some people, the disparity between the punishment and the crime in this case would be evidence for the barbarity of *lex talionis*. But such a case still wouldn't condemn the practice, simply particular (mis)applications.

7. Immanuel Kant, *The Metaphysics of Morals*, trans. and ed. Mary Gregor (Cambridge, UK: Cambridge University Press, 1996), p. 331. The page numbers for Kant's works reflect the standard German edition, *Kant's Gesammelte Schriften*, edited by the Royal Prussian (later German) Academy of Sciences—these page numbers are given in all reputable editions of Kant's works, so that other editions can be consulted.

8. Ibid.

9. Immanuel Kant, *Groundwork of the Metaphysics of Morals*, trans. and ed. Mary Gregor (Cambridge, UK: Cambridge University Press, 1998), p. 429.

10. Ibid., pp. 331–332.

11. G. W. F. Hegel, *Elements of the Philosophy of Right*, ed. Allen Wood, trans. H. B. Nisbet (Cambridge, UK: Cambridge University Press, 1991), p. 124.

12. *Watchmen*, chap. VI, p. 26.

13. Kant, *Groundwork of the Metaphysics of Morals*, p. 332.

14. See Joel Feinberg, "The Expressive Function of Punishment," in *Doing and Deserving* (Princeton, NJ: Princeton University Press, 1974), pp. 95–118.

15. For a good account, see M. Margaret Falls, "Retribution, Reciprocity, and Respect for Persons," *Law and Philosophy* 6 (1987): 25–51. It is odd that Rorschach describes the Comedian's attempted rape of Silk Specter as a "moral lapse." But even if this seems to trivialize the act of rape, it may be indicative of an idea that one bad deed, no matter how heinous, can't remove one's status as a moral agent.

16. For a good account of *lex talionis* and its role in honor cultures, see William Ian Miller, *Eye for an Eye* (New York: Cambridge University Press, 2006).

17. Kant, *Groundwork of the Metaphysics of Morals*, p. 236.

18. Immanuel Kant, *Lectures on Ethics*, ed. Peter Heath and J. B. Schneewind, trans. Peter Heath (Cambridge, UK: Cambridge University Press, 1997), p. 373.

19. Much of the work on honor and Kant was inspired by a paper by Benjamin S. Yost, "Kant's Justification of the Death Penalty Reconsidered," given at the American Philosophical Association's Central Division Meeting, April 2008.

20. Immanuel Kant, *Critique of Practical Reason*, trans. and ed. Mary Gregor (Cambridge, UK: Cambridge University Press, 1997), p. 88.

21. Thanks to Mark White, Bill Irwin, and Ron Novy for their helpful suggestions on early drafts of this chapter.

SUPER-VIGILANTES AND THE KEENE ACT

Tony Spanakos

If the Batman were real, he would be compulsive about eradicating evil, single-minded, and incapable of dealing with moral complexity. He would be, in Alan Moore's words, "a psychopath."[1] In other words, he would be Rorschach—and that is utterly frightening.

What about someone with off-the-charts intelligence like Tony Stark or Reed Richards? Wouldn't someone so smart be tempted to use his or her intelligence to create a utopia, even if that meant sacrificing some people along the way? Enter Adrian Veidt and his plan to bring world peace by eliminating half of New York. In fact, when we think about it, these people who put on masks and costumes and commit acts of violence might be pretty scary if given the chance.

Alan Moore and Dave Gibbons's "superheroes" in *Watchmen* are hardly recognizable to us as "super" or "heroes." Rather than use stereotypical fantasy images of good people who act outside an incompetent criminal justice system, their characters are realistic portraits that challenge the way we look at masked crusaders. *Watchmen*'s heroes raise critical issues about what the government is, who has authority, and how coercion can be used legitimately.

I'm Holding Out for a Hero . . . or a State

Can we really blame the American people in the *Watchmen* universe who passed the Keene Act in 1977, demanding that heroes either register and work for the government or retire?[2] These are the same citizens who reelect President Nixon. But then again, thanks to the intervention of Dr. Manhattan, Nixon won the war in Vietnam, and the Soviet invasion of Afghanistan was not in 1979 but in 1985—at the very moment *Watchmen* takes place.[3] The invasion puts Cold War politics in the microwave, and there are constant apocalyptic symbols in *Watchmen* letting the reader know how grave the situation is. If the world is about to end, isn't this exactly when we need superheroes?

Unfortunately, the characters of *Watchmen* appear old, battle-scarred, emotionally stunted, and morally question-able. Were these really the people who were supposed to save us? Why them? Who gave them their tights and said, "Go forth and bring bedlam to naught"? If these heroes were typi-cal, we probably never would have entertained such thoughts, but Moore and Gibbons's "heroes" force us to reconsider the authority with which superheroes act. In fact, *Watchmen* bril-liantly identifies, explores, and problematizes a very funda-mental tension in the superhero genre, one that has also been central to the study of political philosophy—namely, the legiti-macy of authority.

Different societies have different concepts of legitimacy. In traditional societies, one's status (family/clan, religious, ethnic, class) was the source of authority. An emperor in China was emperor because he was born into a dynastic system. A medi-eval cleric had authority because of the authority invested in the church that ordained him. In modern societies, authority is based less on mystical-charismatic or traditional concepts and more on rationality. This is the argument that German sociologist Max Weber (1864–1920) advanced in the *Theory of Social and Economic Organization*.[4] Although politicians could still rely on the mystical and the traditional for some legitimacy, increasingly, rational arguments needed to be made. This rationality was codified into law, and the application of this law was taken from the hands of priests, nobles, and tribes with "better blood" and given to the state, a bureaucratic apparatus that was supposed to be neutral, offering equal status to all. In such a way, the application of law and punishment was to be rational.

The state used violence in punishing transgressors just as did private groups, such as the Mafia and the Ku Klux Klan. But, unlike those groups, the state's use of violence was legitimate. In fact, in his essay *Politics as a Vocation*, Weber defined the state as "a human community that (successfully) claims the *monopoly of the legitimate use of physical force* within a given territory."[5] The Klan, terrorists, and the common criminal perpetrate acts of violence. But regardless of the justification offered, these acts remain illegitimate—the state alone has the authority to use coercion. People with guns could be bandits or police officers; armed groups committing large-scale acts of violence could be terrorists, rebels, revolutionaries, or soldiers. The difference lies not in the act, but in the authority—the badge, the shield, the uniform, the stripes/stars/what-have-you on the shoulder.

So what about heroes? They definitely have power and use coercion, but they lack authority. The Keene Act is a clear attempt on the part of ordinary citizens to emphasize the authority of the state over the coercive capacity of the superheroes. Are they right? "More than you even realize"—that's the answer coming from *Watchmen*. Departing from the entire superhero genre, it shows why superheroes acting as vigilantes should be terrifying, not emboldening, and justifies efforts to put them under the state's authority as Weber would have liked. Rather than being an intimidating but charming Dark Knight, Rorschach is a psychotically troubled, hideous jingoist, whose use of any means necessary is not employed against superpowered bad guys, but against ordinary people, including the poor and the old. Adrian Veidt is a megalomaniac who reduces the most basic division in international politics to a simple Gordian knot and then commits mass murder for the greater good.

The state's violence *is* more legitimate than Rorschach's and Veidt's. But could heroes work under the aegis of the state? The only *Watchmen* heroes to work for the government are the Comedian and Dr. Manhattan. How well does this work? The Comedian's behavior in Vietnam, on behalf of the state, is anything but heroic. Dr. Manhattan ends the Vietnam War, but he does so with no concern for the lives he has saved or taken. So, *Watchmen* suggests, even under the state's aegis, superheroes aren't necessarily what we would expect and certainly aren't something we should emulate. Perhaps some superheroes can work with the state, but not with the world and the personalities that Moore and Gibbons create. At the very least, there is no guarantee that heroes with coercive power beyond the state will remain loyal to that state.

Working against or outside the State: Rorschach and Veidt

A city is shouting. Claiming that costumed adventurers are making their job impossible, the police are on strike. Everyone is frightened, scenting anarchy.

—Dr. Manhattan, *Watchmen*, chapter IV, p. 22

The Keene Act of 1977 was a reaction to a perceived crisis. The rise of lawlessness and disorder, coupled with the threat to job security that heroes posed to police, led to the criminalization of vigilante activities. Superheroes either had to register and work for the government or retire. Some of the former Crimebusters had already retired (Veidt) and some were already working for the state (Comedian, Dr. Manhattan), but most (like Nite Owl) retired when the Keene Act became law. Only Rorschach refused to recognize the authority of the act.

If Batman, Green Arrow, or some more typical superhero refused to work for the state, he would probably be portrayed as embodying a greater morality than the state, which for reasons of weakness or corruption adopts a lower-order morality. In Marvel Comics's *Civil War* event (2006–2007), in which a similar "Superhero Registration Act" is passed by Congress, the pro-registration superheroes are treated with more empathy than would be expected. But the reader is still pushed toward siding with the renegade heroes. An exchange between S.H.I.E.L.D. Commander Maria Hill and Captain America illustrates the point. When Hill asks him to "handle" the superheroes who will rebel against the act, she says she is asking Captain America "to obey the will of the American people." He responds, "Don't play politics with me. . . . Superheroes need to stay above that stuff or Washington starts telling us who the super-villains are," to which she replies, "I thought super-villains were guys in masks who refused to obey the law."[6] Hill is right. But he is Captain America, a symbol of liberty and justice that is greater than any bureaucrat and perhaps above the particular decisions that a government makes.[7] The superhero genre has taught us to believe our liberty is more likely to be protected by heroes, who are above and beyond the state, than by the bureaucrats who comprise it. Of course, that is usually because those heroes are, well, heroic.

The situation is far less ambiguous with Rorschach, who crafts his response to the Keene Act very strategically, pasting a note that says "never" on a dead multiple rapist left outside police headquarters.[8] In one panel, he expresses the essence of his identity as a superhero in relation to the state: (1) The state is permanently flawed (hence "never," rather than "not until there is a new president"); (2) the state lacks the capacity to execute the law (*he* catches the multiple rapist and dumps the criminal in front of police headquarters as a reminder that "I am doing your job"); and (3) the state lacks the moral clarity necessary for judgment and punishment (he *kills* the criminal, because he sees the criminal as evil by nature, whereas the state won't because it believes in the possibility of reforming criminals).

Rorschach imposes terror in a bar when he breaks the fingers of one patron in order to get information (although he gets none), and later, he uses similar tactics on the very old and retired villain Moloch.[9] Rather than be impressed by his dark nature and willingness to use coercion, the reader is repulsed; maybe that man was once Moloch, but now he is a cancer-ridden old man, whose shriveled body is being contorted by the vicious Rorschach for information.

We may admire Rorschach's devotion to a case that the police are woefully unprepared to investigate, but his methods are—to say the least—suspect. At the same time, Moore and Gibbons's issue is not with the method that Rorschach uses, but with the whole idea of the hero. Would such singular vigilante devotion be okay if it were matched with concern about "human rights"? Most comic books lead us to believe so, but not *Watchmen*. Moore and Gibbons make it clear that even though Rorschach is psychologically deranged, all so-called heroes pose serious problems.

Adrian Veidt, the clean-cut, Ken doll–like former Ozymandias, is actually more terrifying than Rorschach. He is not an immediate and obvious threat to the government. Nonetheless, he hatches his plan to bring peace outside the state. Although Rorschach might be a psychopath, his reach is limited. He muses, "This city is dying of rabies. Is the best I can do to wipe random flecks of foam from its lips?"[10] Meanwhile, Veidt is a megalomaniac who wants to emulate Alexander the Great, the ancient conqueror who ruled almost the entire world "without barbarism."[11] Veidt compares the most basic division in international politics (the Cold War) to the Gordian knot. No one could untie the Gordian knot until Alexander split it with his sword, finding the all-too-simple response to an intractable problem. Veidt believes that the way to end war and human suffering is to force the world powers into aligning against a common enemy (a monster from outer space derived from the imagination of a comic book writer).

Veidt says of Alexander, "True, people died . . . perhaps unnecessarily, though who can judge such things,"[12] and his own plan involves taking the lives of half the city of New York. Rorschach's cruel vigilantism periodically kills criminals in the course of an investigation, but Veidt uses his mind and money to get others to set in motion a plan of mass murder. Clearly, even the less obviously "sick" Ozymandias is also acting in an illegitimate way because he's acting outside the authority of the state. But would a badge have made everything okay? Or, if the state had commissioned his act of "peace," would it be more legitimate?[13]

Working for the Man

So what if superheroes did work for the government? Weber said, "The right to use physical force is ascribed to other institutions or to individuals only to the extent to which the state permits it. The state is considered the sole source of the 'right' to use violence."[14] *Watchmen* falsifies this claim by the very fact that its heroes cannot be assimilated into a Weberian world; that is, even when the state "permits" the use of violence by superheroes, their violence hardly seems legitimate.

Look at Dr. Manhattan's intervention in the Vietnam War. After two months of activities in the country, the disproportionate weapon (Dr. Manhattan) used by one combatant (the United States) compels the other (the Vietcong) to an

early surrender. Dr. Manhattan is analogous to the original
Manhattan Project and the explosion of two atomic bombs in
Japan.[15] It would appear that by Dr. Manhattan's working for
the state, his use of coercion is not only legitimate, but it also
saves countless lives (and restores a sense of invulnerability to
the United States).

But the story of Dr. Manhattan's involvement in Vietnam
does not end there. While in Vietnam, he encounters Edward
Blake, the Comedian, working for the U.S. government. Just
when Dr. Manhattan's presence ends the war, the Comedian's
pregnant Vietnamese lover comes to talk to him about what
will happen next for them as a couple. When Blake tells her
that he plans to forget about her, their child, and her country, she breaks a bottle and slashes his face with it. He then
shoots her. This is shocking, though not as shocking as it
might have been had we not seen the images of the Comedian
in Vietnam, razing the country with a smile on his face. He
tells Dr. Manhattan, "Once you figure out what a joke everything is, being the comedian's the only thing makes sense."
Dr Manhattan asks him, "The charred villages, the boys with
necklaces of human ears . . . these are part of the joke?" to
which Blake responds, "Hey . . . I never said it was a good joke.
I'm just playing along with the gag."[16]

No one considers the Comedian to be a moral pillar; after
all, we know that he forced himself on the original Silk Spectre,
with whom he eventually fathered a child. But the person in
this scene who shocks us the most is Dr. Manhattan. He wit-
nesses Blake about to shoot the Vietnamese woman; he tells
Blake not to do it and afterward says, "She was pregnant. You
gunned her down." Blake replies, "You coulda changed the
gun into steam or the bullets into mercury or the bottle into
snowflakes! You coulda teleported either of us . . . but you
didn't lift a finger!"[17] Indeed, Dr. Manhattan did not lift a finger. Speaking of the Comedian, Dr. Manhattan says, "I have
never met anyone so deliberately amoral. He suits the climate

here: the madness, the pointless butchery. . . . As I come to understand Vietnam and what it implies about the human condition, I also realize that few humans will permit themselves such an understanding. Blake's different. He understands perfectly . . . and he doesn't care."[18]

And yet Dr. Manhattan is so much worse than Blake. He has almost unlimited power, but he has largely separated himself from humanity. In truth, Moore and Gibbons are trying to conceive of what such a powerful being would be like. If a person really had such godlike powers, would he be bound by the same sense of morality that binds us? In *Watchmen*, the result is Dr. Manhattan, who becomes frustrated during a press conference and sends himself into exile, where he creates his own world.[19] He acts like the impersonal god of deists, who creates the world and then walks away—or like an angry kid who picks up his toys and goes home. But . . . just as World War III is about to begin? Just as Veidt is about to destroy half of New York? Clearly, the government cannot control him, nor does his power lead to an obviously good result.

Continuing down this road, Dr. Manhattan does not try to rectify the situation Veidt had wrought, and he actually takes the life of Rorschach, who insists on exposing the plan.[20] After killing the one witness who was willing to protect the common man from a world where "heroes" like Veidt, acting like some deviant version of the philosopher-king, move them around like pieces on a chessboard, Dr. Manhattan walks on the water of the pool in Veidt's mansion, telling Veidt that he plans to go to another, less complicated galaxy. Veidt responds, "I'd hope you'd understand, unlike Rorschach . . . you'd regained interest in human life." Dr. Manhattan's reply is "Yes, I have. I think perhaps I'll create some."[21] Moore is clearly associating Dr. Manhattan with the divine—by his capacities—and yet there is a repugnant amorality about the use of that power. How can he have "interest" in human life after he allowed Veidt to commit mass murder and after he himself committed murder?

Dr. Manhattan is the only character in *Watchmen* who wears neither mask nor costume (nor clothes!) because his identities have become fused. He is also the only one to have superpowers—such incredible powers that men are no more than "termites" to him.[22] At Blake's funeral, he says, "A live body and a dead body contain the same number of particles. Structurally, there's no discernible difference. Life and death are unquantifiable abstracts. Why should I be concerned?"[23] Can people with such powers serve government or even serve their fellow man? There is no question that if the Comedian serves, he does it in a way that is profoundly illegitimate. But Dr. Manhattan is a more subtle reminder that the answer to that question is simply no.

Be Afraid, Be Very Afraid

If you can talk with crowds and keep your virtue, 'Or walk with Kings—nor lose the common touch, if neither foes nor loving friends can hurt you, If all men count with you, but none too much. . . . Yours is the Earth and everything that's in it, And—which is more—you'll be a Man, my son!

—Rudyard Kipling, "If"

Juvenal, a Roman poet in the first or second century, satirized the action of men who found guards to ensure the chastity of their women, asking the very uncomfortable question: "Who will watch the watchmen? The wife plans ahead and begins with them!"[24] Moore and Gibbons pose this question—of how the agent who brings security, if left unchecked, becomes the agent of greater insecurity—within the superhero genre. "Who watches the Watchmen?" is graffitied across New York, appearing at the beginning and the end of the very first chapter and reappearing regularly afterward. When a group of street punks finds out that Nite Owl and the Silk Spectre broke Rorschach out of jail, they answer the question Juvenal and Moore and Gibbons ask.[25] On Halloween, the day when it is socially acceptable for people to open their homes and cookie jars to masked people in costumes, the gang beats Hollis Mason (the sixty-nine-year-old original Nite Owl) to death in a jarringly violent sequence.

Not only is the threat of violence posed by superheroes laid out directly before our eyes in *Watchmen*, but Moore and Gibbons also make clear that the encounter between the masked and the unmasked does not bring risk and violence simply to the latter, but to the former as well. The superhero is Other to the nonsuperhero, different in so many ways. The superhero is able to do what the normal person cannot: what we lack, they have, and what we have, they have in abundance. Dr. Manhattan does not discriminate between live and dead matter, between that which composes men and termites. Not only is that downright scary, but it is likely to inspire vigilantism in normal people as well.

In their highly acclaimed series, *Marvels* (1994), Kurt Busiek and Alex Ross presented the perspective of an everyday reporter who covers superheroes (or "marvels," as he calls them), giving us a worm's eye view of what things would look like if giants truly walked the earth. The results are shocking in that, yes, humans would really be worms in comparison with this new race of beings. And, yes, they would be terrifying to us, even when they performed spectacular acts to save the human race from the planet-swallowing Galactus. How could we ever feel secure when we were surrounded by beings so beyond our physical capabilities? Even the narrator, who is very sympathetic to the marvels and believes that they help normal people, becomes insecure when the mutants appear, especially when he hears Cyclops tell the rest of the X-Men not to fight against the people because "they're not worth it."[26] And thus, insecurity breeds terror, the very thing that superheroes are supposed to quell.

But surely this wouldn't apply to Superman, right? Surely not all-American, Smallville-bred Boy Scout Big Blue, because he is as mindful as anyone of his differences. But Mark Millar and Dave Johnson's Elseworlds tale *Superman: Red Son* (2003) challenged this assumption, asking, What if Superman had landed in the Soviet Union and not the United States of America? The result is frightening. Their Superman continues to be moral (unlike the characters in *Watchmen*), wanting to do good with his powers, defending order and justice. But the problem is that the order and justice are those of Stalin's Soviet Union. When Stalin is poisoned by his son, Superman becomes the new head of the Soviet Union and uses his superpowers and his alliances with Wonder Woman, a reprogrammed Brainiac, and others to engender a utopia in the USSR, a utopia that, terrified of, he eventually leaves behind. The only country not within his power, the USA, is led by a detestable Lex Luthor who is obsessed with defeating the USSR's greatest weapon and leader. Just when Superman is at the acme of his power, he flees in horror at what he has become and the system that he has supported and created.

As *Marvels* and *Watchmen* make clear, the presence of superheroes who constitute an Other to us, almost unrecognizable as humans, should make humans more insecure. *Superman: Red Son* shows how moral superheroes in nondemocratic contexts, in the absence of checks and balances, could similarly tend toward utopia-making activities that have inevitably dystopian results. Ironically, *Watchmen* demonstrates the illegitimacy of immoral and amoral superheroes in a desperate but still democratic United States. But what sort of checks can be put on Superman or any superhero?

Who *Can* Watch the Watchmen?

The lesson of *Watchmen* and the generation of graphic novels it inspired is that as long as superheroes remain in fantastic realms, they are not problematic. But once we place them in reality, once we imagine what the world would be like if they were among us, superheroes stop being such a comfortable concept. The question is not who watches the Watchmen, but who has the *ability* to watch the Watchmen? The superhero's violence will never be legitimate if he or she acts outside or against the Weberian state, but could the superhero truly be bound to the state? Would superheroes truly believe that their authority was borrowed from the state, that the legitimacy of their actions was derived from "registration" with the state, rather than from the very violence that he or she can use? Dr. Manhattan himself says that the government "can hardly outlaw me when their country's defense rests in my hands."[27]

NOTES

1. Alan Moore, "Alan Moore Talks 2: Watchmen—the Superhero Genre," *Comics Britannia*, www.youtube.com/watch?v=qKebCtCTbCA, accessed September 26, 2008.

2. *Watchmen*, chap. IV, p. 23.

3. Ibid., p. 20.

4. Max Weber, *The Theory of Social and Economic Organization*, trans. A. M. Henderson and Talcott Parsons (New York: Free Press, 1947).

5. Max Weber, *From Max Weber: Essays in Sociology*, ed. H. H. Gerth and C. Wright Mills (London: Routledge, 1991), p. 78.

6. *Civil War* #1, July 2006.

7. When Captain America fights the Punisher, Marvel's most bloodthirsty vigilante, the Punisher refuses to fight back because of who Captain America is (*Civil War* #6, December 2006).

8. *Watchmen*, chap. IV, p. 23.

9. Ibid., chap. I, p. 16; chapter II, pp. 21–22.

10. Ibid., chap. I, p. 16.

11. Ibid., chap. XI, p. 8.

12. Ibid.

13. For another treatment of vigilantism in *Watchmen*, focusing on Rorschach and Ozymandias, see Aeon Skoble's "Superhero Revisionism in *Watchmen* and *The Dark Knight Returns*," in Tom Morris and Matt Morris, eds., *Superheroes and Philosophy* (Chicago: Open Court, 2005), pp. 29–41.

14. Weber, *Essays in Sociology*, p. 78.

15. *Watchmen*, chap. IV, p. 20.

16. Ibid., chap. II, p. 13.

17. Ibid., p. 15.

18. Ibid., chap. IV, p. 19.

19. Ibid., chap. III.

20. Ibid., chap. XII, pp. 24–25.

21. Ibid., p. 27.

22. Ibid., p. 18.

23. Ibid., chap. I, p. 21.

24. Juvenal, *Satires*, 6, pp. 346–348. See also "Quis custodiet ipsos custodes?" http://en.wikipedia.org/wiki/Quis_custodiet_ipsos_custodes.

25. *Watchmen*, chap. VIII, pp. 25–28.

26. *Marvels* #2 (February 1994).

27. *Watchmen*, chapter IV, p. 23. The author would like to thank Mark White, Rob Delfino, Michel Spanakos, and Photini The for their comments on a draft of this paper.

SUPERHEROES AND SUPERMEN: FINDING NIETZSCHE'S ÜBERMENSCH IN *WATCHMEN*

J. Keeping

Nietzsche's Super, Man

Friedrich Nietzsche's (1844–1900) *Thus Spoke Zarathustra* fired my imagination with its revolutionary ideas when I first read the book as a young man.[1] The concepts of the will to power, the eternal return, and the revaluation of all values changed the way I looked at, well, everything. But Nietzsche's most compelling, intriguing, and frustrating concept was the "superman," the *Übermensch*, a figure who is capable of feats beyond those of mere mortal men.[2]

Zarathustra—no, not a supervillain, but actually Nietzsche's prophetlike mouthpiece in the book—describes the Übermensch in heroic, not to say superheroic, terms:

I teach you the Übermensch. Man is something that shall be overcome. What have you done to overcome him?

The *Übermensch* is the meaning of the earth.

Behold, I am a herald of the lightning and a heavy drop from the cloud; but this lightning is called *Übermensch*.[3]

Having read *Thus Spoke Zarathustra*, I wanted to *be* an Übermensch, much as in earlier years I wanted to be Spider-Man. But there was a big problem: Zarathustra doesn't directly define what the word Übermensch means, nor does he even attempt to describe what an Übermensch might look like.[4] Some recent commentators think the term refers simply to the "great men" of history whom Nietzsche admired, such as Napoleon.[5] Others see the Übermensch as anyone who has overcome what Nietzsche called the "slave morality" of guilt and resentment.[6]

Although Alan Moore is not a Nietzsche scholar, there can be no doubt that he was acquainted with the philosopher's work; its influence is clear throughout *Watchmen*. And so I propose to draw on the graphic novel to illustrate my interpretation of the Übermensch.[7] I've pretty much given up trying to become such a superman, but you'll have to decide for yourself whether to seek such lofty heights.

God Is Dead, and He's American

Nietzsche's philosophy stems from his famous claim that "God is dead." Of course, Nietzsche didn't literally mean that there was an actual God who was alive and now is not. Rather, what has died is the power of the *belief* in God to sustain a moral order. As science explains more and more of the natural world—including, especially, the origin and development of life—there remains less and less room for God. Science perhaps leaves room for an impersonal agency behind the origin of the universe, but the idea of a personal, caring God who takes an interest in the affairs of humanity is simply no longer as compelling as it once was. The death of God leaves a void in the realm of morality and value: we no longer have a source of objective moral value or of order and purpose in the world.

Rorschach can tell us what a chilling prospect this is:

> Looked at sky through smoke heavy with human fat and God was not there. The cold suffocating dark goes on forever, and we are alone. Live our lives, lacking anything better to do. Devise reason later. Born from oblivion, bear children hell-bound as ourselves, go into oblivion. There is nothing else. Existence is random. Has no pattern save what we imagine after staring at it for too long. No meaning save what we choose to impose. This rudderless world is not steered by vague, metaphysical forces. It is not God who kills the children. Not fate that butchers them or destiny that feeds them to the dogs. It's us. Only us.[8]

This view, that life is essentially meaningless, is called *nihilism*. And it was the desire to find an antidote to nihilism, without returning to the comforting self-deception of objective moral values, that motivated Nietzsche's philosophy. His conception of the Übermensch must be understood as a part of this overall project. At the same time, the dialogue between the naive, black-and-white morality held by characters such as the first Nite Owl and the cynical nihilism of characters like the Comedian informs much of the subtext of *Watchmen*.

What's So Über about the Übermensch?

So we have our first sketch of what it means to be an Übermensch: to be able to look unflinchingly into the abyss of meaningless. And let's face it: how many of us are able to do that, really? Some of us close our eyes and ears to anything that challenges our beliefs. Others concede that belief in God is not rationally justified but nevertheless cling to a half-hearted faith for no reason other than it brings them comfort. Still others give up their faith in God but retain a God-shaped space in their heads, which they fill with an equally unjustified belief in some other objective moral order such as secular humanism. By contrast, the Übermensch not only confronts the moral void head-on, he actually affirms it!

So, is the Übermensch like the Comedian, amoral (without morality), delighting in his most destructive and antisocial impulses? No, but this misunderstanding is natural enough when Nietzsche compares his ideal to the likes of Cesare Borgia.[9]

Nietzsche conceived the Übermensch not as the height of nihilism, but rather as the overcoming of nihilism. Consider Zarathustra's parable of "Three Metamorphoses," wherein the spirit becomes first a camel, then a lion, and finally a child.[10] The camel represents the stage whereby we take values seriously and are committed to them. The lion represents the nihilist, who rejects and rebels against the values that he once held dear. But the lion is only a step on the way to the child, who creates new values. The creation of new values is the end and the goal of this progression.

So, the Übermensch is a creator of new values. But what does this mean? For our purposes here, values can refer to moral *rules* ("Thou shalt not kill"), as well as to actions and qualities that are considered to have value. In this second sense, then, truthfulness and loyalty could be values (both are examples that Nietzsche himself cites). Values of this kind might instead be called *virtues*. But we can value things other than virtues: we can value freedom or comfort, for example. In their argument on Mars, Laurie has to persuade Jon that human life has value (itself an important Nietzschean theme). Thus, to create values could mean to create rules of human conduct or to posit certain things as worth promoting or protecting. Of these, Nietzsche was concerned primarily with the latter. Indeed, he rejected morality in the form of a table of "Thou shalt nots" as impoverishing and life-denying.[11] Instead, he hoped that the death of the old God might make room for values of affirmation, new ways of making life worth living.

How might we go about doing this? We cannot look to the origins of our existing values for help, because they were created in a religious or otherwise metaphysical context. We don't want to simply repeat the mistakes of the past by creating new law tables whose foundations are no more secure than those that are in the process of collapsing. To overcome nihilism, we must create values *without* foundations, values that are freely chosen within, rather than putatively imposed from the outside. As Rorschach puts it, we must "scrawl [our] own design on this morally blank world."[12] Of course, we cannot simply posit values *arbitrarily*—I can't suddenly resolve to value stuttering and cruelty to animals. Instead, the values we create must be somehow compelling, if not to others, then at least to ourselves.

Nietzsche seemed to think that we create values by creating *ourselves*. And by creating oneself, Nietzsche meant more than just choosing a name and an associated image, as each of Moore's superhero characters do. Instead, Nietzsche called for a commitment to a particular way of life.

Indeed, it makes sense to link the creation of values with the creation of a self. If we're to hold a value with integrity and commitment, as opposed to giving it mere lip service, then we must *live* it. We must allow it to inform our lives such that we incorporate it into our thoughts, actions, and attitudes.

The Nietzsche Method

Unfortunately, Nietzsche didn't have a step-by-step guide on how to create oneself—if he had, perhaps he could have

marketed it, as Ozymandias does with "the Veidt Method"—
but Nietzsche did give us some hints. On the topic of the
Übermensch, Zarathustra proclaims, "I taught them all *my*
creating and striving, to create and carry together into One
what in man is fragment and riddle and dreadful accident."[13]
This recalls a passage from Nietzsche's earlier book *The Gay
Science*, in which he spoke of "giving style":

> *One thing is needful.* "Giving style" to one's character—a
> great and rare art! It is exercised by those who see all the
> strengths and weaknesses of their own natures and then
> comprehend them in an artistic plan until everything
> appears as art and reason and even weakness delights the
> eye. Here a large mass of second nature has been added;
> there a piece of original nature has been removed: both
> by long practice and daily labor. . . . In the end, when
> the work is finished, it becomes evident how the con-
> straint of a single taste governed and formed everything
> large and small. Whether this taste was good or bad is
> less important than one might suppose, if only it was a
> single taste![14]

If we are justified in bringing these passages together, it
sounds as if an Übermensch is one who has taken himself
up as a project and trained his mind and body into a harmonious and integrated whole. Elsewhere, Nietzsche spoke of
a "dominant thought" or a "ruling idea" that motivates the
creator, which resonates closely with the "single taste" mentioned previously.[15] If we understand the "ruling idea" as that
which governs this reconstruction of one's character, and if we
identify it with the value (or values) that one creates, then the
Übermensch is a person who creates a value by organizing his
or her character in a coherent way around this value, by making it the formative principle of his or her life.

So did Nietzsche have in mind someone like Rorschach, lacking friends or interests, single-mindedly pursuing his objective

to the exclusion of all else? I don't think so. Nietzsche's ideal was someone who possessed "all the strong, seemingly contradictory gifts and desires—but in such a way as they go together under a yoke."[16] That is, he meant a person with a plurality of talents and interests, but who had them under control, so that the person could focus his or her time and energy in a specific direction, rather than being pulled in all directions.

Nietzsche seemed to think that we cannot find life worth living unless we attach some meaning to it. Without God to impose meaning from the outside, we must create this meaning for ourselves. But if this meaning is to be powerful enough to sustain a life, it can come only from a commitment of our whole selves to a project. Someone who can do this stands as an exemplar of a particular value or way of life and may inspire others, thereby "giving meaning to the earth."

In an interview, Adrian Veidt asserts, "By applying what you learn and ordering your thoughts in an intelligent manner it is possible to accomplish almost anything."[17] Is this so? Could you or I become an Übermensch? Or does it take a very special kind of person? Nietzsche seemed to believe the latter, claiming, "Never yet has there been an Übermensch."[18] But perhaps it is a goal worth aspiring to.

Who Watches the Übermensch?

We now have a rough idea of what Nietzsche meant by the Übermensch and why he considered the concept so important. Armed with this knowledge, we can turn to the cast of *Watchmen* and see whether any of them come close to Nietzsche's ideal. We'll be limiting our discussion to the characters whose personalities and backgrounds are fairly well fleshed out in the story: the two Nite Owls (Hollis Mason and Dan Dreiberg), the Comedian (Edward Blake), Rorschach (Walter Kovacs), Ozymandias (Adrian Veidt), Dr. Manhattan (Jon Osterman), and both Silk Spectres (Sally and Laurie Juspeczyk).

There may be some very interesting tales to tell about Mothman and Captain Metropolis, but since Moore did not choose to tell them, we cannot discuss them here.

As we've noted, there's more to creating oneself than just making up a name and putting on a costume. Hollis Mason, for example, comes across very much as, in Rorschach's words, "just a man in a costume." His autobiography makes it appear that he launched on his superhero career because "it was fun and because it needed doing and because I goddam felt like it."[19] In fact, since he was already working as a cop, it appears to be simply an extension of his existing persona and not a new persona at all. Mason's autobiography also makes it clear that he never seriously questioned his values or beliefs; instead, his masked adventures were motivated in part by the simplistic religious morality he received from his grandfather. Finally, donning his costume was an act of imitation; as he puts it, "dressing up in a costume and protecting your neighborhood had become something of a fad."[20] Clearly, the first Nite Owl does not meet any of the criteria for an Übermensch.

The second Nite Owl is a more psychologically complex character than his predecessor. Although he presents himself as a rich boy who took up adventuring more out of boredom than anything else, there's a strong sense that his costumed persona constituted for him a kind of self-realization. We see Dreiberg as a fairly impotent individual, both literally and figuratively, until he once more dons his costume in chapter VII. Whereas the first Nite Owl was very much the same man in or out of costume, the second Nite Owl appears to be more himself in the costume than out of it. Hesitant and self-doubting as Dan Dreiberg, he is confident and assertive as Nite Owl. What makes the character most interesting, however, also distances him from the ideal of the Übermensch, the self-created individual who has disciplined himself into a harmonious whole.

This is because Dreiberg's superhero career appears to be tied up with a dimly grasped sexual repression. This is evident from the sexually charged atmosphere of the fight against the muggers in chapter III, from the dream in chapter VII, and from his ability to overcome his impotence by having sex in costume (also in chapter VII), where he first acknowledges the connection between sex and his superhero proclivities. Although there is certainly nothing damning about sexuality from a Nietzschean point of view, the fact that Dreiberg fails to comprehend, let alone integrate, this aspect of his personality causes him to fall short of the standard of wholeness required of an Übermensch.

Sally Juspeczyk embarks on a crime-fighting career in a mercenary attempt to promote her modeling career. Her superhero identity is therefore not so much a persona as a pose. Sally's daughter, Laurie, by contrast, never chose to embark on a superhero career at all. Instead, she was pushed into it by her mother and happily gave it up when the Keene Act once more made vigilantism illegal. Obviously, neither Silk Spectre is a serious candidate for an Übermensch.

Laurie's father, the Comedian, however, presents a more interesting case. Although Blake may have created himself in the image of a brutal, meaningless world, his pose as a comedian makes him ultimately unable to affirm anything. Blake's laughter is of the mocking sort, which denigrates, rather than celebrates, its subject matter. (Think here of the distinction between laughing *with* and laughing *at*.) Although he has confronted nihilism, he is unable to move beyond it. This is what motivates his costumed career: unable to create, he instead takes pleasure in destruction, and being a superhero gives him license to do so.

And Then There Were Three . . .

This leaves us with Rorschach, Dr. Manhattan, and Ozymandias. For each of these characters, there's some reason to think they might approximate the ideal of the Übermensch. Consider

Rorschach. More so than any of the other characters, he has looked into the abyss of nihilism and has been transformed by it. Furthermore, he is perhaps the most committed to his superhero persona, viewing it as his "true self" and Kovacs as his "disguise." Nothing matters to him except his work: "There is good and there is evil, and evil must be punished. Even in the face of Armageddon I shall not compromise in this."[21] Could Rorschach be an Übermensch?

I think not. As I hinted earlier, Rorschach resembles more the self-impoverishment of an obsessive than the harmonious whole that characterizes an Übermensch. It's also puzzling that Rorschach should speak of good and evil when he asserts elsewhere that this world is "morally blank." It appears that Rorschach isn't strong enough to face the death of God after all. Looking at the abyss only causes him to cling more tightly to his conservative values, despite the fact that he no longer has any right to them. This is evident throughout the book, culminating in his insistence on unveiling Ozymandias's hoax and thereby undoing all the good that it has accomplished, for the simple reason that "evil must be punished." Whereas the Comedian remains stuck in the nihilism of the lion, Rorschach reverts from the lion back into the camel. Rorschach does not affirm, he *denies*. And this is why there is an element of *malice* in his morality, as when he says, "The accumulated filth of all their sex and murder will foam up about their waists and all the whores and politicians will look up and shout 'Save us!' And I'll look down and whisper 'No.'"[22] Perhaps this is the real reason Rorschach refuses to help Veidt save the world—because he hates it.

So, what of Dr. Manhattan? He creates himself in a far more literal sense than any other character when he rebuilds a body for himself after being disintegrated in the accident that grants him his powers. And in contrast to Rorschach, he appears to give up the belief in objective values, asserting that "life and death are unquantifiable abstracts."[23] But although

Dr. Manhattan is the most powerful character in *Watchmen*, he is also paradoxically the most ineffectual. His origins do not lie in a choice but in an accident. Interested only in scientific research, he allows himself to be controlled by others. "The newspapers call me a crimefighter, so the Pentagon says I must fight crime."[24] Later he intervenes in Vietnam, a conflict he has no interest in, again on governmental orders. And his unique view of time saddles him with a fatalism that drains all motivation from his life. Never really choosing anything, he is quite literally just "going through the motions." As such, he is neither creative nor life-affirming.

In the end, though, Jon does (finally!) break out of his complacency by affirming the value of human life in his argument with Laurie on Mars and by choosing to support Veidt's hoax by killing Rorschach—his first really decisive act since becoming Dr. Manhattan. Shortly thereafter, he leaves the story, and Earth, planning to create human life of his own. This is more promising, but creating life with God-like powers is still something quite different from being the Übermensch, who creates a way of life and affirms it despite all mortal limitations. I think we can do better.

And so we come to Ozymandias. No superhero epic is complete without a criminal mastermind. And with startling originality, Moore presents us with a criminal mastermind who is at the same time one of the heroes. More so than any of the other characters, Veidt consciously sets out to create himself. His exceptional intellect invests him with a sense of destiny but without providing a specific goal. He begins by giving away his fortune, so that he can start from nothing. Then he journeys through Europe and Asia, acquiring knowledge and skills, and later trains himself to be an exceptional athlete. Of all of the characters, he gives the strongest impression of having ordered his body and mind into an "artistic plan." He even creates and markets the Veidt Method as a means of doing so. Although it's not evident whether he acknowledges the death of God, insofar as he commits an act of mass murder in order to achieve what he sees as a greater good, he certainly places himself "beyond good and evil."[25] Although Ozymandias presents his vast scheme in altruistic terms, it's impossible to overlook a level of megalomania in his words and actions, especially when he compares himself to the likes of Alexander and Ramses II. His creative act is not to create only himself, but an entire world order; in so doing, he can certainly be described as "giving meaning to the earth."

Do We Have a Winner?

Of all the characters in *Watchmen*, Ozymandias most closely resembles Nietzsche's Übermensch, but even here the resemblance is not complete. Although by committing mass murder he appears to break with conventional morality, his actions simply conform to *utilitarianism*, which endorses the principle that "the end justifies the means."[26] Nevertheless, I believe that Ozymandias is a close approximation of what Nietzsche meant by the Übermensch.

It is interesting to note that the character who comes closest to Nietzsche's ideal is the villain of the piece. But although Ozymandias is a mass murderer, he is not a conventional villain, and most of the characters who learn of his plan come to accept, if not approve of, it.[27] Moore has stated, though, that the protagonist of the pirate tale presented inside *Watchmen* is meant to represent Veidt.[28] If this is so, then this unnamed character's descent into murder and madness can be seen as a commentary on Veidt's actions, which suggests that Moore does not at all approve of or endorse them.

We need not, however, agree with Moore in this evaluation. Nor are we required to side with Nietzsche by seeing the Übermensch as a good thing. Whether the Übermensch is an ideal worth aspiring to or a dangerously amoral monster is something each of us must decide for ourselves.

NOTES

1. *Thus Spoke Zarathustra*, originally published in complete form in 1892, is available in *The Portable Nietzsche*, trans. Walter Kaufmann (New York: Viking Penguin, 1968). *Zarathustra* resembles an epic poem as much as it does a philosophical treatise. Nietzsche's contemporaries were used to the dry disseminations of Immanuel Kant and G. W. F. Hegel and had no idea what to think of it. It is composed primarily of speeches by the eponymous character but also includes episodes in a sort of loose narrative. The language is florid and evocative; to many readers, it sounds like the Bible.

2. There is no universally accepted English translation of the German word *Übermensch*. Although it was initially translated as "superman"—and this is how that word entered the English language—Walter Kaufmann preferred the term "overman" in his translations, which have subsequently become standard. Later Nietzsche commentators have also employed *overperson* or *overhuman*. Given these inconsistencies and the fact that Nietzsche uses the word as a technical term, I have chosen to leave it in the German.

3. *Zarathustra*, pp. 124–126.

4. As you can imagine, this led to much misunderstanding about the concept. Most early readers took it in Darwinian terms, as signifying the next step in human evolution. Then came the Nazis, who misappropriated Nietzsche's philosophy and attempted to create a "master race" of Übermenschen through selective breeding.

5. See, for example, Daniel Conway, "The Genius as Squanderer: Some Remarks on the *Übermensch* and Higher Humanity," *International Studies in Philosophy* 30 (1998): 81–95.

6. Mathias Risse, "Nietzsche's 'Joyous and Trusting Fatalism,'" *International Studies in Philosophy* 35 (2003): 147–162, would be an example of this view.

7. My interpretation is indebted to those of Walter Kaufmann in his *Nietzsche: Philosopher, Psychologist, Antichrist* (Princeton, NJ: Princeton University Press, 1950), and Arthur Danto in his *Nietzsche as Philosopher* (New York: Columbia University Press, 1965).

8. *Watchmen*, chap. VI, p. 26. Rorschach's language here echoes that of Nietzsche when he first announces the death of God; see *The Gay Science*, trans. Walter Kaufmann (New York: Vintage, 1974), p. 181.

9. Ruthless Italian general and statesman, the son of the famously corrupt Pope Alexander VI, and one of the models for Machiavelli's *The Prince*. The comparison can be found in Nietzsche's *Ecce Homo*, p. 261.

10. *Zarathustra*, pp. 137–140.

11. For an extended discussion of why Nietzsche thought this, see his *On the Genealogy of Morals*.

12. *Watchmen*, chap. VI, p. 26.

13. *Zarathustra*, p. 310.

14. *The Gay Science*, p. 232.

15. *Zarathustra*, p. 175.

16. Friedrich Nietzsche, *The Will to Power*, trans. Walter Kaufmann and R. J. Hollingdale (New York: Random House, 1967), p. 446.

17. *Watchmen*, chapter XI, supplemental material, "After the Masquerade: Superstyle and the Art of Humanoid Watching," by Doug Roth, p. 9.

18. *Zarathustra*, p. 205.

19. *Watchmen*, chap. I, supplemental material, "Under the Hood," by Hollis Mason, p. 5.

20. Ibid., chap. II, supplemental material, "Under the Hood," by Hollis Mason, p. 7.

21. Ibid., chap. I, p. 28.

22. Ibid., p. 1.

23. Ibid., p. 21.

24. Ibid., chap. IV, p. 14.

25. Nietzsche's phrase and the title of one of his books.

26. For more on utilitarianism, see chapter 5, "Means, Ends, and the Critique of Pure Superheroes," by J. Robert Loftis.

27. It is worth noting that Nite Owl, Silk Spectre, and Dr. Manhattan become complicit in Veidt's scheme only *after the fact*. If they had known of it in advance, they likely would have tried to stop it.

28. This interview can be found at www.blather.net/articles/amoore/watchmen3.html. The parallel between Veidt and the tale of the Black Freighter is also indicated in one of Veidt's own speeches: "I dream about swimming toward a hideous . . . no, never mind" (*Watchmen*, chap. XII, p. 27). This is evidently a reference to the end of the tale, in which the protagonist realizes the horrors that he has committed and swims to the freighter to join the crew of the damned.

PART TWO

THE VEIDT PLAN: *WATCHMEN* AND ETHICS

MEANS, ENDS, AND THE CRITIQUE OF PURE SUPERHEROES

J. Robert Loftis

Near the climax of *Watchmen*, Rorschach and Nite Owl confront Ozymandias in his Antarctic fortress, and Ozymandias starts explaining his insane plan, which will perhaps save the world, but at the cost of millions of lives. While the smartest man in the world is offering up the last crucial bit of plot exposition, Rorschach looks for a weapon. He can find only a fork, but he tries to stab Veidt with it anyway. Ozymandias blocks the blow and sends Rorschach to the floor, all the while continuing his monologue. After Rorschach gets up, he tries to make another move on Ozymandias but is blocked by Bubastis, the genetically engineered supercat. Ozymandias doesn't even need to turn to face Rorschach, let alone miss a beat of his monologue. Not sure what else to do, Rorschach tries talking: "Veidt, get rid of the cat." "No I don't think so," Ozymandias replies magnanimously. "After all her presence saves you the humiliation of another beating."[1] Ozymandias's speechifying is a great foil for the taciturn Rorschach. An even starker contrast comes when Veidt is finally confronted by someone more powerful than he—Dr. Manhattan, the comic's only true superhero. While Rorschach doggedly attacked a foe he knew he couldn't beat, Ozymandias immediately suggests compromise. If the others stay silent, they can enjoy the benefit of Veidt's new world. Everyone accepts the compromise—after all, they can't undo the attack on New York—except Rorschach, even though it means his certain death.

The contrast between the two characters' willingness to compromise shows a deep divide in their underlying ethical worldviews. Ozymandias appears to be what philosophers call a *consequentialist*: he believes that all actions should be judged by their consequences, implying that the ends will sometimes justify the means. He is the kind of guy who, when he has to make a decision, carefully lists the pros and cons and goes with the option that has the most pros on balance. At least, that's the way Ozymandias thinks of himself. Consequentialism is how Ozymandias rationalizes the bizarre murderous scheme that was revealed in the Antarctic fight. But consequentialism has a long and noble philosophical tradition, and the great consequentialists of the past would certainly disavow Ozymandias as one of their own.

Rorschach, on the other hand, appears to be a *deontologist*. Deontology says that we should not think of morality in terms of ends and means at all; instead, we should act only in ways that express essential moral rules. Rorschach deontologically rationalizes his actions, such as stabbing away at Veidt using anything he can find, even though he knows he can't succeed. The outcome doesn't matter; what matters is doing the right thing. But deontology also has an old and noble philosophical tradition, and the great deontologists of the past would certainly disavow Rorschach as one of *their* own. Acting to express moral rules does not mean seeing the world in black and white.

As the chapters in the book you're holding show, *Watchmen* is an intensely philosophical comic, and concepts like consequentialism and deontology were clearly on Alan Moore's and Dave Gibbons' minds as they created the book. I hope to show that their attitude toward both consequentialism and deontology in *Watchmen* is profoundly negative. Yet these are actually only stepping-stones to the real point of *Watchmen*. The ultimate target of the comic's critique is *authoritarianism*, the idea that anyone should set himself or herself up as a guardian of society. Superheroes serve as the images of power and authority in *Watchmen*. The ideologies that the heroes pretend to follow are rationalizations of that power, and the corruption of the superheroes serves as a critique of both power and its rationalizations.

"'In the end'? Nothing ends, Adrian, nothing ever ends."

When Ozymandias is being chased by Dr. Manhattan, he lures Manhattan into an intrinsic field gizmo (like the one that first created the big blue man) and activates it, which seems to zap Manhattan into vapor, disintegrating Ozymandias's beloved kitty Bubastis in the process. Afterward, Ozymandias says offhandedly, "Hm, you know, I wasn't really sure that would work."[2] (Actually, it didn't.) This is a great Veidt moment in a couple of ways: it shows his willingness to make big sacrifices for even bigger ends, and to gamble on probabilities. He doesn't deal with a world of black and white, of evil and good, as Rorschach does. Everything is gray, but some gray areas are darker than others. To do the right thing, Ozymandias simply chooses the lightest shade of gray.

In the history of philosophy, this sort of weighing, calculating consequentialism is most associated with the doctrine of *utilitarianism*. Although the basic idea behind utilitarianism has been around forever, the doctrine didn't really begin to flourish until the work of the English philosophers Jeremy Bentham (1748–1832) and John Stuart Mill (1806–1873). The core idea is simple: "actions are right in proportion as they tend to promote happiness, wrong as they tend to produce the reverse of happiness."[3] Utilitarianism is built from consequentialism by adding elements, as one adds ingredients to a soup. The first new ingredient is *hedonism*: the good that one is trying to maximize in the world is happiness. The utilitarian is not worried, as Rorschach is, about being sure that every criminal is punished. Punishment is only a good policy if, as a consequence, it makes someone happier by preventing future crime. The other new ingredient is *egalitarianism*. Everybody's happiness is weighed equally. Thus, if an action will make five people happy and one person unhappy (all by equal amounts), you should do it, even if the one unhappy person is your mom—or your favorite genetically engineered cat.

Now, utilitarians are well aware that one cannot in advance know which things will really maximize happiness for all. So most utilitarians don't recommend that we simply try to calculate the best possible outcome each time we make a decision. Instead, we should rely on the rules and habits that the human race has developed over time for acting morally. Thus, the version of utilitarianism that is appropriately called *rule utilitarianism* says that one should live by the rules that would maximize happiness for everyone if they were followed consistently. So Veidt might adopt a rule for himself such as "Never kill," not because killing never brings more happiness than unhappiness, but because a person who lives by such a rule would generally bring more happiness than unhappiness.

The version of utilitarianism called *virtue utilitarianism* asks you to develop the personal characteristics that are likely to maximize happiness for all if you really made them a part of you. Thus, Veidt could spend his time developing a sense of compassion, because compassionate people generally bring more happiness than unhappiness to the world.

Utilitarianism has had many critics over the years, and it looks like Moore and Gibbons are among them. We can see this first of all in the structure of the story. According to the standard comic book formula, Rorschach is the hero of the story and Ozymandias is the villain (though, of course, nothing is really that simple in *Watchmen*). Rorschach is the first person we see, and the plot is structured around his investigation of several murders. The audience uncovers the truth behind the murders as Rorschach does. Ozymandias, on the other hand, is behind the murders, and when he is found out, he reveals his elaborate plot involving the further death of millions. Ozymandias also has one of the key flaws that marks comic book villainy: he is a megalomaniac who wants to take over the world. He may say that the purpose of his plan is to "usher in an age of illumination so dazzling that humanity will reject the darkness in its heart."[4] But we know the first thing he thinks about when he sees his crazy scheme succeed is his own glory. "I did it!" he shouts, fists in the air. And he immediately begins planning his own grand role in this utopia.

If Ozymandias is the villain, then perhaps utilitarianism is a villain's ideology. It certainly looks as if consequentialism contributed to his corruption by allowing him to rationalize self-serving ends and blinding him to the profound injustice of what he has done. The potential for consequentialism to promote rationalization is obvious: once one starts in making sacrifices and trade-offs, it gets easy to make the sacrifices that will serve one's own interest. The deeper harm that consequentialism seems to have brought, though, is letting Veidt believe that he can *force* people to sacrifice their well-being—indeed, their lives—for the greater good. Veidt thus fails to consider basic justice or fairness. Is it fair that the citizens of New York are forced to sacrifice their lives and sanity to end the Cold War, when no one else is asked to make such a sacrifice? The means for preventing this kind of unfairness is typically the doctrine of human rights, which tells us that there are some things the individual cannot be asked to do against his or her will, even if it is for the greater good. One of the most common criticisms of consequentialist doctrines such as utilitarianism is that they are unable to embrace a doctrine of universal human rights. And in *Watchmen*, we certainly see the consequences of failing to take the rights of New Yorkers seriously.

The Utilitarians Strike Back

At this point, utilitarians will object that they are being unfairly maligned. Veidt is at best a parody of the ethic they recommend. Far from rationalizing self-serving interests, utilitarianism is the least selfish doctrine around, because one's own happiness counts no more than anyone else's. As Mill wrote forcefully, "I must again repeat, what the assailants of utilitarianism seldom have the justice to acknowledge, that the happiness which forms the utilitarian standard of what is right in conduct, is not the agent's own happiness, but that of all concerned."[5] More important, utilitarians would object that their theory does indeed allow for justice and human rights. Mill was a passionate defender of liberty and an early advocate for women's right to vote, so it was very important for him to argue that utilitarians can account for justice. He did this by using the tools of rule utilitarianism: to make decisions effectively, individuals and societies must adopt rules for themselves. Experience shows that individuals and societies that recognize rights are more likely to maximize happiness than are those that don't. If Veidt had been a real utilitarian, he would have recognized this and adopted stricter rules about killing people.

Moore and Gibbons don't address these nuances—as we shall see in the last section of this chapter, they are primarily interested in showing ethical theories as ways of rationalizing power. They do, however, offer another critique of utilitarianism that can't be dealt with by adjusting the fine points of doctrine. It is important to note that the critique doesn't come from the alleged consequentialist Veidt but from Dr. Manhattan. In one of the most moving sequences in the book, Veidt asks Manhattan, with unexpected plaintiveness and insecurity, whether he's really the good guy he thinks he is: "Jon, before you leave . . . I did the right thing, didn't I? It all worked out in the end." In the next panel, we see Dr. Manhattan from Veidt's point of view. The blue man, standing inside a model of the solar system, arms down, palms out, smiles and says, "'In the end'? Nothing ends, Adrian. Nothing ever ends."[6] Then he leaves Earth for good. Dr. Manhattan's warning is borne out four pages later, when we see Seymour, the inept assistant at the *New Frontiersman*, reaching toward Rorschach's journal looking for something to fill up space in the next issue. If he grabs it, Veidt's scheme could be ruined, and all that suffering would be for nothing.

Utilitarianism asks us to look to the future and sum up the consequences of our actions, but the future is infinite, and you can't crunch the numbers when every one of them turns to infinity. Perhaps in five years something will happen that undoes the good that Veidt did. Then, ten years after that, something good will happen that could only have happened given Veidt's actions. The problem here isn't just that we can't know the future, but that there is too much of it. Even if we had an infinite mind to encompass the infinite future, what would we see? An infinity of happiness and an infinity of suffering? We can't do anything to change a ratio of infinity to infinity.

And even if we could, what of it? Utilitarianism gets its motivation from the basic instinct that pain is bad and pleasure is good. Individually, you and I seek pleasure and avoid pain. Utilitarianism tries to remove the selfishness of this by asking us to seek pleasure for everyone. In doing so, it tries to make ethics a little more objective: less about what *you* want and more about what is good in itself. But if we keep going with this impulse to objectivity, everything loses its meaning. What does it matter if there is more pain or more pleasure in the world? We are now in the perspective of Jon Osterman after his accident: if you take too abstract a perspective, nothing seems valuable at all. This is a defect in Ozymandias's world-view. Unlike other characters—Rorschach or the Comedian—Ozymandias has never really confronted the question of the meaning of life or the possibility that life is meaningless. All of his personal revelations are about the source of suffering in the world, not about the possibility of morality. He learns that evil is not just a matter of crime, but comes from geopoliti-cal forces. But he never questions the nature of evil and good itself. This is the real significance behind Moore and Gibbons's decision to name this character Ozymandias and to use the Shelley poem as the epigraph to chapter XI. Ozymandias takes a bigger view but never the biggest view.

"Even in the face of Armageddon I shall not compromise in this."

So Ozymandias is a tragic villain, a man whose overwhelming ego and failure to appreciate the dark nature of life led him to think the end can sometimes justify the means. That means Rorschach is the hero, right? Well, no. Rorschach is a foil for Veidt in every respect: the unkempt, taciturn, right-wing out-sider against the slick, eloquent, left-wing celebrity. But just being a mirror to the villain doesn't make you the hero.

As we saw earlier, Rorschach often uses deontology to rationalize his actions. We see this in his constant mantra "in the face of Armageddon I shall not compromise," which is an echo of the deontologists' slogan: "Let justice be done, though heaven should fall."[7] Deontology goes beyond saying that the ends never justify the means. It actually says that at least in moral decisions, you shouldn't think in terms of ends and means, or consequences, at all. Once you start thinking about means and ends, you've left the realm of morality altogether, because you're only thinking about how to get something you want, either for yourself or someone else. According to deontologist Immanuel Kant (1724–1804), morality begins with the good will. Anything else you might value in life—intelligence, strength, even happiness itself—can be used for evil. The only thing good, really, is the *will* to do good, the mental act that says, "I am going to do the right thing."

By the same token, if you are doing something solely to achieve some end, you are not doing it because it is the right thing to do. This applies not only to ends we think of as selfish, but even to those we think of as ethical. Think about a cruel and selfish act, like the Comedian shooting his pregnant Vietnamese girlfriend at the end of the war. A deontologist would think that part of why this is wrong is because of the Comedian's motivation. He's not trying to do what is right; he's merely trying to accomplish an end that is convenient for him, getting rid of a person as if she were extra baggage. Now think about an unselfish act, such as the redemptive moment at Bernard's newsstand when so many passersby intervene to break up the fight between Joey and her girlfriend Aline. If one of them was jumping in simply to make himself look good or even to feel good for helping somebody, that would simply be acting for an end. But if someone helped because it was the right thing to do, even if that person had no desire to do so, that tells us that his or her act was moral (in a deontological sense). Interestingly, the people who intervene don't talk about pity; they give more deontological explanations, such as, "It's all that means anything."[8] They have to act because they're moral people in a dark world that can only be lit by the good will. They're doing the right thing because it's the right thing. Kant would smile.

But Rorschach is not a hero, and his deontology is not Kant's. It is a shadow of deontology that is used to rationalize fascist thuggery. I wish I could show this simply by pointing out that Rorschach is a psychotic killer, but in comics, as in Hollywood, crazy vigilantes have a certain cachet. To see the real problems with Rorschach and his use of deontology, we need to look at his hypocrisy, the way his deontology degenerates into "dichotomous thinking," and his failure to recognize the intrinsic value of persons.

Rorschach is not only a flat-out hypocrite, but his hypocrisy reveals his real commitments. Rorschach's supposed commitment to deontology takes a back seat to the need to project strength in the face of moral decline. Although he delivered the announcement that he ignored the Keene Act on the dead body of a serial rapist, he shows admiration for the Comedian, who attempted to rape the first Silk Spectre and confessed to having done many other "bad things to women."[9] After trashing Moloch's apartment, Rorschach says, "Sorry about the mess, can't make an omelet without breaking a few eggs," a classic bit of consequentialist reasoning.[10] To heighten the irony, Moore and Gibbons even depict him stealing a raw egg from Moloch's fridge, carefully cracking it open, and drinking it. Rorschach also professes admiration for President Harry Truman, because Truman was willing to sacrifice the lives of millions in Hiroshima and Nagasaki in order to avoid even bigger losses in the war—basically the same trade-off Ozymandias makes.[11] The pattern behind all of these exceptions is telling. In each case, Rorschach slips into consequentialist reasoning in order to justify a hypermasculine display of power and violence. This shows that his real worldview is simply fascist. All of the elements of classical fascism are there: obsession with moral decline, idolizing the masculine and fearing the feminine, and belief that democratic authority has failed and must be replaced with something more direct.[12]

A deeper abuse of deontology comes in Rorschach's obsessive *dichotomous thinking*, the mistake of looking at the world in black and white. Rorschach is thus guilty of committing a *fallacy*, a mistaken but very tempting way to reason. *Watchmen* goes out of its way to show that where Veidt could at least see shades of gray, Rorschach is a simple dichotomous thinker. His initial attraction to the fabric he made his mask from, for instance, came from the fact that black and white never mixed.[13] Rorschach seems to think that dichotomous thinking comes with deontology. All of his statements of deontological principles also say that he sees the world in black and white: "There is good and there is evil and evil must be punished, in the face of Armageddon I shall not compromise in this."[14]

But dichotomous thinking is not at all a part of deontology. Kant taught that we should not do things for the sake of ends, but for the sake of doing the right thing. Still, this does not mean that "the right thing" has to be something simpleminded or rigid. For Kant, doing the right thing meant obeying what he called the "categorical imperative," a rule he phrased a couple of different ways. The first was to "Act as though the maxim of your action were to become, through your will, a universal law of nature."[15] This sounds weird, but it is really just asking you to remember a question your mother asked you as a kid: "What if everyone did that?" For instance, if you pinched some candy from the drugstore, Mom probably said something like, "Listen, honey, I know it seems like no one is hurt, but what if everyone shoplifted candy? The store would go out of business and then no one would have any candy." Using a universalization test like this allows for much more subtle ethical reasoning than Rorschach is capable of. What if everyone was a crazed vigilante who punished every infraction with death?

The biggest reason Rorschach is not a real deontologist is that he fails to show respect for persons. Earlier, we said that Veidt's worldview fell short of being moral because he failed to recognize rights, the moral rules that prevent us from sacrificing an individual for the greater good. Kant captured this in the second formulation of his categorical imperative: "Act in such a way as to treat humanity, whether in your own person or in that of anyone else, always as an end and never merely as a means."[16] Again, this sounds weird, but what it boils down to is "Don't treat people like mere tools to achieve your ends." When Veidt destroys New York, he is using the city's inhabitants as tools for ending the Cold War, thus violating their basic rights as persons.

Rorschach likewise fails to recognize the rights we typically grant people—for example, the right to a fair trial. Really, Rorschach drew the wrong lesson from his existential moment burning down the home of that child butcher. According to Kant, we are obligated to always respect the basic rights of persons, because only a person is capable of exercising a good will, and a good will is the only thing that is truly good. Rorschach saw some of this as he "looked at the sky through smoke heavy with human fat."[17] He saw an existentialist version of Kant's claim that the only thing good is the good will. In Rorschach's version, "existence is random, save what we imagine after staring at it too long" and therefore we are "free to scrawl our own design on a morally blank world." What Rorschach didn't see, but Kant did, is that this requires us to respect the people who are capable of scrawling a moral design on the world.

"Who watches the watchmen?"

So, neither consequentialism nor deontology comes off well in *Watchmen*. The characters use the ideas as thin rationalizations for corrupt behavior, and, at least in the case of utilitarianism, the ideas themselves are shown to be flawed. But critiquing consequentialism and deontology is not the main goal for Moore and Gibbons. Their deepest concern is obviously expressed in the aphorism that gives the comic its name and that appears in fragmentary form throughout the book: "Who watches the watchmen?" The line finally appears in full form at the very end of the book, but in a strange way. Moore and Gibbons give the original source, Juvenal's *Satires*, but then mention that it is quoted as the epigraph of the Tower Commission Report (which resulted from investigations of the Iran-Contra scandal during President Ronald Reagan's administration). This is a detail people tend to pass over, if only because the report was written before many current readers of *Watchmen* were even born. Perhaps this obscure bit of 1980s history appears only because Moore and Gibbons were reading the newspapers, rather than Latin poetry, during the era of Reagan and Thatcher. And the poem in which the line originally appears is about the difficulty men have keeping their women in line—a bit of patriarchy that is not a big concern for the comic. The Tower Commission, on the other hand, is exactly the sort of thing the comic is about.

Watchmen depicts an alternate universe in which the Watergate scandal never takes place, a man with superhuman powers allows the United States to win the Vietnam War, and Nixon is now in his sixth term in office, thanks to a new constitutional amendment. Covert criminal activity of the sort the Tower Commission exposed seems to have driven this history: Moore and Gibbons strongly imply that the Comedian assassinated Woodward and Bernstein and further hint that in this world, Nixon and the Comedian were involved with the Kennedy assassination. Ultimately, this is all intended as a warning about how a free society can collapse into authoritarianism, something Moore had previously depicted in *V for Vendetta*.[18] In that comic, he showed England sliding into fascism after limited nuclear exchanges in Africa and the European continent, followed by environmental and economic collapse. In 1988, when DC Comics reprinted a colorized run of the series (including the ending, which had gone unpublished because the magazine it ran in originally was canceled), Moore wrote a melancholy introduction lamenting the power of Thatcher's Tory Party. Given what has happened, he realizes he was mistaken to believe that "it would take something as melodramatic as a near-miss nuclear conflict to nudge England toward Fascism."[19] Basically, Moore was not satisfied with the picture of a decline of a democracy into authoritarianism in *V*, and *Watchmen*, which was first serialized in 1986, is in part a correction of this.

Ozymandias and Rorschach are a crucial part of this picture, since the superheroes in *Watchmen* are images of authority. Moore told the BBC program *Comics Britannia* that "What *Watchmen* became was entirely a meditation about power. We were thinking about how to some degree each of these characters represented some sort of power."[20] Rorschach and Ozymandias are important because we see in them that anyone can be corrupted. Leftist or rightist political views are really of little consequence, because they are merely ways that the powerful rationalize what they are doing. Consequentialism and deontology are merely further rationalizations of these ruling ideologies. It is thus not surprising that neither view really gets a fair shake in *Watchmen*. Moore and Gibbons aren't interested in whether the views can be tinkered with to the point that they are a reasonable guide to behavior, because that is not how these ideologies function in the real world. Notice also that the most moral characters in the comic, the two Nite Owls, are basically nonideological. They don't have big moral ideas but rather rely on a basic sense of decency (as described in the next chapter of this book). Dreiberg, the second Nite Owl, specifically shies away from making grand decisions that affect the whole world because one person simply isn't competent to do so.[21] The real lesson behind the entire comic is that no one, no matter what his or her ideology, should be entrusted with too much power.[22]

NOTES

1. *Watchmen*, chap. XII, p. 9.

2. Ibid., p. 14.

3. John Stuart Mill, *Utilitarianism*, 7th ed. (London: Longmans, Green, and Co., 1879), chapter 2. Available (free) at www.gutenberg.org/etext/11224.

4. *Watchmen*, chap. XII, p. 17.

5. Mill, *Utilitarianism*, chap. 2.

6. *Watchmen*, chap. XII, p. 27.

7. Rorschach offers many variations on the "never compromise" mantra. The two that come closest to the deontologists' slogan given previously are *Watchmen*, chap. I, p. 24, and chap. XII, p. 20.

8. Ibid., chap. XI, p. 20.

9. Ibid., chap. II, p. 27; chap. VI, p. 15; and chap. II, p. 23.

10. Ibid., chapter V, p. 6.

11. Ibid., chap. VI, supplemental material, Walter J. Kovacs case file, excerpt of an essay by Walter J. Kovacs.

12. Umberto Eco, "Ur-Fascism," in *Five Moral Pieces*, trans. Alastair McEwen (New York: Harcourt Trade, 2002), pp. 65–88.

13. *Watchmen*, chap. VI, p. 10.

14. Ibid., chapter I, p. 24.

15. Immanuel Kant, *Groundwork for the Metaphysics of Morals* (1785), trans. Jonathan Bennett (2005), online at www.earlymoderntexts.com, Second Section. This quote appears on p. 421 of print editions (with standard Academy pagination).

16. Ibid., p. 429.

17. *Watchmen*, chap. VI, p. 26.

18. Alan Moore and David Lloyd, 1982–1985, *V for Vendetta* in *Warrior*, issues 1–26 (Brighton, UK: Quality Communications).

19. Alan Moore and David Lloyd, *V for Vendetta* (New York: Vertigo, 1988), p. 6.

20. BBC Bristol, *Comics Britannia* (2007), www.bbc.co.uk/bbcfour/comicsbritannia/comics-britannia.shtml; click on "Alan Moore Interview II."

21. *Watchmen*, chap. XII, p. 20.

22. For more on this theme, see chapter 3 in this book, "Super-Vigilantes and the Keene Act," by Tony Spanakos.

THE VIRTUES OF
NITE OWL'S POTBELLY

Mark D. White

One reason *Watchmen* has captivated readers for more than twenty years is its fantastic cast of characters, most of whom can be both disarmingly realistic and unbelievably over-the-top at the same time. Of course, I'm not talking about Dr. Manhattan, the one true "superhuman" in the series—he's hardly realistic. Mostly, I'm talking about Ozymandias and Rorschach, the megalomaniacal genius and the psychopathic vigilante of the group. They impress us with their heroic intentions and devotion but at the same time disturb us with their moral extremism. Not surprisingly, they're the characters who get the most attention (including in the preceding chapter in this book).

In this chapter, I want to focus on the "everyman" of *Watchmen*—Dan Dreiberg, the second Nite Owl. He is definitely a hero, as Ozymandias and Rorschach are, but otherwise he is nothing like them. He's a brilliant scientist, but not on the level of Adrian Veidt. He can take care of himself in a fight, but nothing like Rorschach. And, let's face it, when he decides to defy the Keene Act and don the tights again, he's not exactly in peak physical condition (though the Silk Spectre hardly seems to mind). He's an ordinary guy in an extraordinary world, doing good without ruining himself in the process. And that, I shall argue, makes him the most *virtuous* of the heroes in *Watchmen*.

Watchmen and Virtue? (Hurm . . .)

As the previous chapter detailed, Ozymandias can be connected with the ethical theory of *utilitarianism*, while Rorschach is closer to a particularly dark brand of *deontology*. I maintain that Nite Owl is an ideal hero from the viewpoint of *virtue ethics*, particularly the classical virtue ethics of Aristotle (384–322 BCE).

Virtue ethics, dating from the days of the ancient Greeks (and perhaps earlier), stands in contrast to utilitarianism and deontology in two significant ways. First, virtue ethics relies on rules differently in providing moral guidance. For instance, both utilitarians and deontologists would say that (in most cases) killing another person is wrong, but for different reasons. The utilitarian would consider the net effects on happiness and would condemn killing unless it could be shown that total happiness was increased, which will happen in only the rarest cases. (This, of course, was Veidt's argument for his "psychic bomb," a rare case if ever there was one!) Utilitarians follow a rule of maximizing happiness, and any act that passes this test is moral. On the other hand, the deontologist would say that killing is wrong (in most cases) because of something inherently wrong in the act itself, regardless of its consequences. Various deontologists would have different reasons for this, but all would say there is a general rule of "Do not kill."[1]

Virtue ethicists (advocates of virtue ethics) condemn killing as well, but not only because it breaks a rule as such. In addition, they would say that murder or unjustified violence of any kind is a vice, the opposite of a virtue. Virtue ethicists *describe* the act, rather than evaluate it with a rule. Of course, you can easily turn a virtue or a vice into a corresponding rule. If murder is a vicious act, then the appropriate rule would be—three guesses—"Do not murder." But calling something a virtue or a vice is not based on a rule for or against it—rather, the rule comes from being a virtue or a vice.[2]

This leads us to another unique aspect of virtue ethics: its focus on the person more than on the act. I previously said that virtue ethicists describe the act itself, but it would be more accurate to say they describe the person performing the act. Even more precisely, virtue ethicists would comment on the *character* of the person acting. Murder itself is a bad act, of course, but virtue ethics would also emphasize the viciousness of the *murderer.* A generous person has a charitable character and is virtuous (at least, in that aspect). This point allows us to refine a virtue-based rule: "do what a virtuous person would do," which translates into "perform virtuous acts." But, whereas utilitarians and deontologists evaluate acts without referencing the person doing them, virtue ethics emphasizes the actor and evaluates him—his acts provide evidence of his underlying character.

Rorschach, Meet . . . Forrest Gump?

Virtue ethics sounds all well and good, but one thing seems to be missing—who's to say what counts as a virtue? On the surface, it seems like something Forrest Gump might have said—"virtue is as virtuous does"—but that doesn't help much, does it? Some virtues seem easy to pick out: honesty is good, right? Kindness, courage, loyalty: they're all good. Is that all we have to do, pick out character traits we happen to think are good? What if other people picked out different ones?

In fact, different virtue ethicists do pick out different virtues for different reasons, but in this chapter we'll focus on one of the original virtue-oriented philosophers, Aristotle. To Aristotle, a virtue in general helps something perform its function well; the virtue of a horse, for example, "makes the horse excellent, and thereby good at galloping, at carrying its rider and standing steady in the face of the enemy."[3] So, for human beings, a virtue is a character trait that leads to performing well, which to Aristotle meant living a good, full, flourishing life.

Okay . . . so what does it mean to flourish, to lead a full life? (It seems like the goalposts keep moving back, doesn't it?) "Flourishing" is a common translation of Aristotle's term *eudaimonia*, which is also often translated as "happiness." But he didn't mean happiness as in "Wow, a new X-box!" or "Wow, an Ozymandias action figure!" If we're going to use the word *happiness*, we have to make clear that we mean "real" or "true" happiness, a deep, meaningful, long-lasting fulfillment of the soul, not a trivial, passing moment of pleasure. This is why *flourishing* is the preferred term among the "cool" virtue ethicists; it has that sense of a full life that gets better over time through self-improvement and growth.[4]

And what's more, virtuous actions do not lead to happiness or fulfillment but are actually the source of it: "In general, what expresses virtue pleases the lover of virtue. Hence their life does not need pleasure to be added as some sort of ornament; rather, it has its pleasure within itself."[5] This does not mean that the virtuous person cannot enjoy "ordinary" pleasures like the rest of us. Rather, it simply means that acting virtuously is also a pleasure to him or her, and a distinctly different sort of pleasure at that. Think of doing a crossword puzzle. Is most of the enjoyment in seeing the finished puzzle or in the process of solving it? Even if you don't finish it, you still had fun. In a similar way, "virtue is its own reward," as they say (especially if it fits into a crossword).

Nite Owl in the Middle

So what sets Nite Owl apart in the virtue department? He's a hero, and heroism is surely a virtue (as are all of the character traits involved in being a hero), but Ozymandias and

Rorschach are heroes, too. Out of the three of them, however, only Nite Owl leads a life that flourishes, a full life, a life that isn't self-defeating. Ozymandias may seem fulfilled—he has a huge Arctic mansion, gets every TV channel (at once!), and has nice pets and lots of servants. But at the same time he's obsessed with improving the world, and obsession—even regarding a good end—is never virtuous, for it does not help one flourish. Rorschach is even more obsessed—and given his childhood, who can blame him? But we're not dealing with blame or responsibility here, only with the choices that a person makes that determine the state of his or her life. More clearly than with Ozymandias, I think we can agree that Rorschach does not flourish—his is a life none of us would emulate (more on that later).

But Nite Owl is a normal guy—aside from being a costumed vigilante, that is. Why does that make him more virtuous than Ozymandias or Rorschach? Because Nite Owl strikes a balance between the extremes of the other two, and that balance is a key aspect of Aristotle's definition of virtue. To Aristotle, virtue "is a mean between two vices, one of excess and one of deficiency."[6] If you pursue any character trait too much or too little, you are not acting virtuously. Only by striking the balance, or the mean between the two extremes, are you exhibiting virtue. (Of course, once this mean has been found, you can't practice it too much. You can't be too moderate!)

Almost any character trait that we might generally consider a virtue can be taken too far or not far enough. For instance, consider bravery, which Aristotle discusses at length.[7] Bravery involves having the right amount of fear in a situation and acting appropriately. A person who has too much fear and shrinks from doing the right thing is called a coward or a chicken (with apologies to the chicken lobby). A person who has too little fear and rushes into the fray is foolhardy or rash. Although we often admire such people—after all, Daredevil and Green Lantern are both known as heroes "without fear"—in most cases in the real world (outside the military, where it has instrumental and strategic value), such an attitude is pretty foolish. ("Fools rush in," they say.) The virtuously brave person, then, displays courage in the face of danger, unlike the coward, but knows enough to consider other options when the danger is too great (and more likely lives to face danger another day).

In chapters VII and VIII of *Watchmen*, we see Dreiberg's brave nature, first in saving the victims of a tenement fire, then in deciding to break Rorschach out of prison. He is deliberate but not headstrong; he is cautious but not foolhardy. We can contrast his behavior with the Silk Spectre's, who joins him in these endeavors but makes clear that she does it more for the excitement and to make up for the boredom of her sequestered life with Dr. Manhattan. She is even more cautious than Dan is and refers to busting Rorschach out of jail as "insanity" and risky, though no one would call her cowardly.[8] At the other end of the spectrum, we have—of course—Rorschach, whom Laurie calls reckless (as if there were any doubt).[9]

And it's not just bravery—Nite Owl displays many other virtues described by Aristotle: mildness, friendliness, and wit, just to mention a few.[10] Can we apply any of these terms to either Rorschach or Ozymandias? Aristotle contrasts mildness to anger—Rorschach is definitely on the high end of the anger scale, while Ozymandias doesn't seem to get angry at all, even upon being ambushed by Nite Owl and Rorschach in chapter XI. Friendliness? Rorschach has only had one friend (Nite Owl), while Ozymandias seems to be above having friends altogether. (Nite Owl, of course, may as well be the Mr. Rogers of the *Watchmen* universe.) And although Dan Dreiberg is no comedian (or Comedian), he has an easygoing sense of humor that eludes the other two: Rorschach is too twisted, whereas Ozymandias is too serious. In all of these ways, Nite Owl is nicely in the middle, striking the mean between the extremes.

Mama, Don't Let Your Babies Grow Up to Be *Watchmen*

Another important concept in Aristotelian virtue ethics is the *moral exemplar*, a person who embodies many or most of the virtues we would like to have. Moral exemplars—or role models, as we would call them today (sorry, Ari)—are particularly useful for children, who can often get their moral training more easily through imitating and emulating their role models than through memorizing and applying abstract rules and principles.

Moral exemplars or role models are often people whom you know, such as parents, teachers, or religious leaders, or maybe famous people such as athletes, performers, or government leaders. But they can also be historical figures, such as George Washington, Martin Luther King Jr., or Gandhi. The idea is that you choose a person who exhibits the virtues you would like to see in yourself, and you try to emulate the choices that person would make in a given situation. If this is successful, at first you will be imitating the virtuous character of your role model, but over time you will develop those virtues yourself.

Now, let's get back to *Watchmen*. Ask yourself: if you were to pick one of the three characters we've been discussing to be your moral exemplar—or, better yet, your kid's role model—who would it be?[11] I'm pretty sure Rorschach's out—do we even have to discuss him? Ozymandias, in contrast, does have many good qualities but takes some of them to the extreme. Now, exhibiting an extreme devotion to something does not rule you out as a role model. Star athletes train much longer and harder than most of us ever will, but we can still hold them up as role models, as something to strive for, even if the ultimate end is unattainable. But Ozymandias is so extreme in so many ways, as explained in chapter XI (his "origin issue"), and many of his actions and choices are so questionable, that he would not make a good role model.[12]

Out of the three characters we've been discussing, Nite Owl clearly makes the best role model or moral exemplar. He is a good guy, plain and simple. He's brave but not foolhardy. He helps people, but he does so carefully and thoughtfully. He's loyal to his friends but not to the point of servility. He displays all of the virtues we've discussed, striking the mean between the extremes, and that is why he makes a better role model or moral exemplar than either Ozymandias or Rorschach. (Seriously, was Rorschach even in the running for this?) This is not to say that Nite Owl is perfect or that he exhibits *all* of the virtues—he could do a few more crunches, and there's the worrisome costume fetish, too—but no one is perfect, and that includes people we may hold up as moral exemplars.

Are We Wasting Our Time Discussing Character and Virtues?

Okay, let's say you accept what I've said so far, that Nite Owl exhibits virtuous character traits, yada yada yada. But what exactly does it mean to "exhibit a character trait," virtuous or not? For instance, what do we mean when we say that Hollis is honest or that Gloria is sweet?

Well, most simply, we can say that a person with a certain character trait can be expected to act accordingly most of the time. When we say that Hollis is honest, we may mean that he will tell the truth when it is expected of him. We don't expect him to be honest in every situation—no one is perfectly honest, just as no one is perfectly virtuous in any way. But obviously, if someone tells the truth more often than not, or in cases where there is a greater temptation to lie or fib, we would judge that person to be more honest.

But that doesn't seem enough, does it? Does it matter *why* Hollis is behaving honestly? He could tell the truth because he believes that will get him further in life or that he will be punished in the afterlife if he doesn't. In other words, his honesty is somewhat tainted by its motivation. Knowing this, we may not even say any more that Hollis is honest, just that he is very practical.

True honesty seems to require more—not only that a person behaves honestly, but that he *is* honest himself. His honesty must be a part of him, an essential ingredient of his character. He doesn't tell the truth for opportunistic, self-serving reasons but instead because it is who he is. What's more, he values honesty in others, and he is particularly attuned to situations that challenge the ideal of honesty. All of this still doesn't guarantee that he will tell the truth perfectly in every case—everyone slips—but when he does (or doesn't), it isn't a matter of rational calculation.

All three of our characters have the general character trait of heroism, expressed in completely different ways, and none of them seem to be heroic for the wrong reasons. (But only Nite Owl's heroism is virtuous for the reasons we've discussed.)

Do people really have character traits in this sense, though? Can we really say that Hollis is *essentially* honest or that Gloria is *essentially* sweet—or could it be simply that we have not seen them behave otherwise? Maybe they just haven't been pushed hard enough, or we have observed them only on a good day? Are we making too big a deal out of patterns we see in people's behavior? How well do we *really* know people, anyway—especially comic book characters?

All of these questions are part of a recent challenge to virtue ethics known as *situationism*, which argues that people's behavior at any given time is determined more by the specifics of that particular situation than by any general character traits. The most forceful argument for situationism is made by John Doris in his book *Lack of Character: Personality and Moral Behavior*, in which he presents a wealth of experimental evidence for his case.[13] Many of the studies reported in his book show people's altruistic behavior being affected by seemingly meaningless factors, such as whether they happen to find change in a payphone before they have a chance to help someone. If people did have robust, reliable character traits, Doris claimed, then such irrelevant details of a particular situation would not affect people's behavior so strongly.

Needless to say, virtue ethicists have not taken Doris's book (and other related work) sitting down.[14] Instead, they've stood up and made several arguments in their defense. For instance, they've said that character traits, especially virtuous ones, cannot be captured by simple observed behaviors, but involve essential parts of a person that we only occasionally glimpse through her behavior. Honesty, as we know, is more than just telling the truth—it is a part of the person herself, one that manifests itself in truth-telling behavior but actually involves much more. Also, they've argued that all of the experiments Doris cited involve changing the nature of the situation, which obviously may lead to a change in behavior, whereas character traits deal more with consistency in any one given situation over time. And there is always more than one virtue at play in any given situation, so what Doris interpreted as a lapse in one virtue may really be another virtue that the person is acting on instead.[15]

What does this all mean for *Watchmen*? If you side with Doris, you believe that calling Nite Owl brave (in a moderate, virtuous sense) or Rorschach paranoid and obsessed (in every sense) is casting far too wide a net over a handful of observations of their actions. The situationist would argue that if Nite Owl found himself in Rorschach's shoes, he would behave much as Rorschach did (and vice versa). But if you find this hard to swallow—that, for instance, Nite Owl would have broken a man's fingers one by one to extract information from him, as Rorschach did—then you have reason to doubt Doris's analysis, and you may give some credit to virtue ethicists' belief in consistent character traits.[16]

Dan, Dan, He's Our Man!

Although Rorschach may be the most compelling character in *Watchmen*—and Ozymandias is definitely the shiniest—Dan Dreiberg, the humble Nite Owl, is the most virtuous. Out of the three, he lives the most fulfilled life, a truly flourishing life. I mean, the man fights crime *and* writes for ornithology journals! He was Rorschach's one-time friend and partner but escaped the faceless one's joyless, reckless lifestyle. And if your kids were to have a *Watchmen* poster on their wall, you know you would want it to be of Nite Owl. (Suck in that gut and say cheese, Dan!)[17]

NOTES

1. Again, see chapter 5 of this book, "Means, Ends, and the Critique of Pure Superheroes," by J. Robert Loftis, for more on these two ethical systems and their relationships to Ozymandias and Rorschach.

2. Rosalind Hursthouse, a modern virtue ethicist, argues that virtue ethics is no more or less rule-oriented than utilitarianism or deontology is, because all three systems based their rules on some underlying moral concept, such as utility, rights, or virtue. See her book *On Virtue Ethics* (Oxford: Oxford University Press, 1999), chap. 1. (Much of what I write in the first half of this chapter is influenced by her defense of traditional virtue ethics.)

3. Aristotle, *Nicomachean Ethics*, trans. Terence Irwin (Indianapolis: Hackett Publishing, 1985), p. 1106a. (These page numbers are standard for referencing Aristotle's work and should appear in any reputable edition.)

4. As you can imagine, virtue ethics is often criticized for not being precise enough. (No, really!) But again, we can easily argue that utilitarianism and deontology have their own areas of vagueness as well. What's "utility"? What counts as "right" or "wrong"? Every question leads to more, no matter what ethical system you choose. (That's what keeps philosophy professors flourishing.)

5. Aristotle, *Nicomachean Ethics*, p. 1099a.

6. Ibid., p. 1107a.

7. Ibid., Book iii, chaps. 6–9.

8. *Watchmen*, chap. VIII, p. 4.

9. Ibid., p. 20.

10. All are discussed in *Nicomachean Ethics*, Books iii and iv.

11. On the question of whether a fictional character can serve as a moral exemplar, see Ryan Indy Rhodes and David Kyle Johnson, "What Would Batman Do? Bruce Wayne

as Moral Exemplar," in Mark D. White and Robert Arp, eds., *Batman and Philosophy: The Dark Knight of the Soul* (Hoboken, NJ: Wiley, 2008), pp. 114–125.

12. This is assuming that we know everything about him; presumably, he is quite the role model in the *Watchmen* universe, judging from all the Ozymandias merchandise available!

13. Cambridge, UK: Cambridge University Press, 2002.

14. For the literature discussing Doris's arguments, see http://moralpsychology.net/jdoris/?page_id=7. For an application of his argument to comic book characters (namely, Iron Man and Batgirl/Cassandra Cain), see my "Do Superheroes Lack Character?" at http://comicsprof.blogspot.com/2007/03/do-superheroes-lack-character.html.

15. One of the best critiques of Doris's book is Gopal Sreenivasan's 2002 article "Errors about Errors: Virtue Theory and Trait Attribution," *Mind* 111, pp. 47–68.

16. *Watchmen*, chap. I, p. 16.

17. My sincere thanks go to Jennifer Anne Baker, who graciously offered detailed comments regarding virtue ethics.

RORSCHACH: WHEN TELLING THE TRUTH IS WRONG

Alex Nuttall

Rorschach's Death

Near the end of *Watchmen*, we discover that Adrian Veidt, aka Ozymandias, has successfully completed his plot to murder millions of people in order to bring about world peace. Laurie Juspeczyk (the Silk Spectre), Dan Dreiberg (the second Nite Owl), and Dr. Manhattan then make a pact with Veidt to conceal what he has done. If they revealed the truth, as Dr. Manhattan explains to Laurie, it would "destroy any chance of peace, dooming earth to worse destruction. . . . If we would preserve life here, we must remain silent."[1] Rorschach, however, abstains:

> Dreiberg: Rorschach. . . ? Rorschach, wait! Where are you going? This is too big to be hard-assed about! We have to compromise. . . .
>
> Rorschach: No. Not even in the face of Armageddon. Never compromise.[2]

Rorschach, being single-minded in his pursuit of justice (or his sense of it, at least), has no concern for what might happen if he reveals Veidt's conspiracy. And, indeed, Manhattan atomizes him. Though it's somewhat unclear why Dr. Manhattan kills Rorschach, it's obvious that an essential element of Dr. Manhattan's choice to do so is a concern over what would happen if the world found out about Veidt's actions.[3] We are led to believe that Veidt's plot is somewhat successful (although we don't know how long it will last). If Rorschach had been allowed to tell the world of the plot, then perhaps the world peace that resulted would not have occurred. In other words, maybe the world would be *worse off* if Rorschach had his way. Laurie Juspeczyk and Nite Owl are in agreement with Dr. Manhattan that the world should not find out (although, unlike Manhattan, they aren't willing to kill Rorschach to make sure of that).

These circumstances make for great story-telling, sure, but they also pose a difficult moral question: can it be wrong or immoral to tell the truth?

Lying for the Sake of Humanity

As a culture, we typically believe that lying is wrong. But that's just in theory—when we're given specific cases, we may come to different conclusions. In other words, we often bend, or even break, the rules when it comes to lying. Imagine, for instance, you're protecting someone from Big Figure, a known murderer. Big Figure knocks on your door and asks you if you know where the person you are protecting is hiding. What should you do in these circumstances? Most people would say that *obviously* you should lie to him. Likewise, Laurie Juspeczyk and Dan Dreiberg decide to lie (or at least refrain from talking) about Veidt's plot. Their situation is extraordinary and beyond our experience. But we can make sense of why they thought that in their particular situation lying was called for and that telling the truth would have been the morally wrong choice.

Not everyone accepts the view that we should lie to the hypothetical "murderer at the door." Immanuel Kant (1724–1804) and some of his supporters have argued that lying is *never permissible*, not even if a murderer is asking for where you are hiding his potential victim (recall Rorschach's unwillingness to compromise, mentioned previously).

Why did Kant think this? He insisted that we should all "act in such a way that you treat humanity, whether in your own person or in the person of any other, always at the same time as an end and never merely as a means."[4] This principle, one of the versions of Kant's *categorical imperative*, tells us that if we ever use someone only as a "mere means" to achieve our own agenda, we have violated that person's essential dignity. For instance, Veidt lies to the writers, the artists, and the scientists on his secret island in order to complete his plan. According to Kant, Veidt would be wrong for doing so, because each of those writers, artists, and scientists is what we call a "rational agent"—any being who can reason, make decisions, and is responsible for those decisions. Rational agents should not be wronged, according to Kant, because they are beings of "absolute worth" or dignity.

It is not obvious why we should consider rational agents as having absolute worth, but it does seem that we think rational agency to be very important. Part of the tragedy of an event like the one at the end of *Watchmen*, where millions of people die, is more than the sheer loss of life. Millions of bacteria die every day, and we don't usually find this cause for concern—in fact, we are more concerned with the creation of bacteria! What *is* important is the type of life that is lost. Human lives have more value than other types of life because we make decisions and we reason. That is not to say that other types of life aren't important, because they certainly are. We often think a lot is at stake when considering a human life (and, presumably, any type of life if it can make decisions and reason).

When we lie to rational agents, we are failing to respect their true worth. We are taking away their decision-making powers because when we lie to them, we are trying to get them to do or think something they wouldn't if we told them the truth. We are manipulating them and we are treating them as *mere means*, rather than as beings who possess an inviolable dignity. According to Kant, this is never okay. And if we accept that every rational agent is a being of absolute worth, it's difficult to see why we shouldn't agree with Kant.

But Is Lying Really That Big a Deal?

So, while Kant's theory seems to fit well with our beliefs about the worth of humans or rational agents, it doesn't fit well with our beliefs about lying. We believe we should lie to the murderer at the door looking for the person we are hiding inside. It seems that we would believe that lying is *morally required* in this circumstance. Also, we would think that someone who told the truth to the murderer is callous, heartless, and an immoral person for doing so.

The problem with the murderer-at-the-door situation is that it involves a conflict between our duties. A *duty* is what is morally required of us, derived from Kant's imperative that we should never treat someone as a mere means. Here the conflicting duties are the duty to not lie and our duty to protect people from undue harm. According to Kant, however, our duties never conflict. If duty is what morality requires of us, then, logically, two duties cannot both be required if only one can possibly be followed. It would be as if Veidt both *did* and *did not* transport a monster into New York, where it killed millions—only one event can be true. For duties required by the categorical imperative, it is the same: there is only one duty that is the right one for any situation.

What *can* conflict, according to Kant, are the *grounds of obligation*, the reasons we have to think that a particular duty is the one we should follow. The specific reasons we have for performing the conflicting duties can lead us to different conclusions about what we should do. So, in the murderer-at-the-door situation, we do not have a conflict of duties but a conflict of the grounds of obligation. We have reasons to protect the person we are hiding in our house and we have reasons to not lie. But, according to Kant, only one set of reasons leads to the correct action. What is actually our duty, in any given circumstance, is always singular—there is always and only one correct action for that circumstance. And it does not seem unreasonable to believe that the more important obligation is to save a life, not to refrain from lying.[5]

Kant seemed to believe, however, that the correct action is not to lie to the murderer at the door.[6] We can better understand Kant's position against lying to the murderer at the door by considering two points. First, according to Kant, there are some things we simply cannot do to stop a murderer, such as torture him. Torture, like lying, involves an assault on a rational agent's will and as such treats the person as a mere means. Torturing someone is a much more tragic event than lying is, but, according to Kant, both acts are wrong for the same reason—both treat the person as a mere means.[7]

A second consideration that shows that Kant's position isn't as rigid as it seems is his belief that we can't be held responsible for the actions of others. So, if you decide not to lie to the murderer and the murderer goes ahead and kills the victim hiding in your house, it is not your fault that he did so. It is the murderer's fault. Yes, you could have done something to stop him, but Kant claims that the blame properly lies at the murderer's feet. Thus, according to Kant, telling the truth can't be considered immoral, even though it leads to serious harm (for which you are not responsible).[8]

So what should we conclude about the ethics of truth-telling in Rorschach's case? Remember, Rorschach is not trying to protect a victim he's hiding from Veidt—Veidt has already killed his victims. Rorschach is just trying to expose the truth, with the consequence that the emerging world peace may crumble. Although he does have a duty to not lie, he has no duty to tell the truth. And while it seems like a common-sense requirement that he not say anything, it does not seem as if he is morally required to stay silent. So, it would be difficult to say that Rorschach is *required* to tell the truth, as he seems to think, but neither can we say that he is required to stay silent. After all, the blame for what follows would lie at the feet of Veidt; if the truth becomes known to the public through Rorschach's morally valid actions, we can't hold him responsible for the consequences. So it would seem that, at least from a Kantian point of view, Rorschach should not be considered morally wrong if he tells the truth about Veidt's scheme.

Utilitarianism: A Justification for Lying?

Not everyone is a Kantian, however—try convincing the editor of this book of that—and there are other important ethical theories to consider.[9] *Utilitarianism*, with its focus on the results of actions, rather than on the actions themselves, gives us a different evaluation of Rorschach's actions.[10]

For example, let's consider white lies. Imagine that Laurie tells occasional white lies to her mother, Sally, such as saying, "Wow, Mom, you look great in your old Silk Spectre costume!" Laurie lies in order to avoid a damaging emotional conflict with her mother (because their relationship is already fairly tense). And we can probably remember countless situations where we did something similar. In cases in which we think telling white lies is acceptable, we are aiming to achieve the most pleasure over pain, consistent with classical utilitarianism.

We all respect the importance of being honest, but in such situations, honesty can prove more costly than it's worth. Perhaps part of the equation is that in such situations we are expected to be polite, and being polite often means saying something positive. If we instead decide to reveal our negative feelings, then we are breaking the rules of decorum and we are therefore doing more than just expressing our feelings. We are perceived, instead, to be issuing an attack, which can be much more damaging to our relationships with others. Thus, telling white lies allows us to avoid such situations. This generic type of utilitarianism would also allow us to lie for many other reasons, not simply to cover up our dislike of someone's fashion choices.

We can see how, on the surface, utilitarianism seems to offer more flexibility when it comes to lying than Kantian ethics does. Things might be different, however, if we consider another type of utilitarianism. Typically, when we discuss utilitarianism, we are talking about *act utilitarianism*, which focuses on the results of each individual act—for example, Veidt's decision to murder millions of people to secure world peace. *Rule utilitarianism*, on the other hand, focuses on the overall results of a certain way of behaving, instead of on particular acts. Although occasional lies may be okay, in general we realize that lying has negative consequences. But since it is often hard to tell which cases are which, it is easier just to follow a rule of not lying, as this rule will lead to the best consequences averaged over time. So we should always follow this rule, even in cases where it may *appear* that breaking the rule would indeed maximize happiness, because we may never be sure that *this* time it will be okay.[11]

What do rule and act utilitarianism tell us about Rorschach's choice to tell the truth? Act utilitarianism might tell us that Rorschach would be wrong for telling the truth. I say "might" because it all depends on what the consequences of that action would be. Nite Owl and the others believe that telling the truth would result in a net balance of pain over pleasure, which would make the action definitely wrong. But a case can always be made that the world would actually be a better place if Rorschach were to tell the truth. For example, we could argue that even though there would be turmoil following the revelation that Veidt murdered millions of people, the world would be better off knowing the truth. Perhaps knowing the truth would be a deeper or more authentic pleasure that would outweigh the world peace brought about by lies. Or maybe the world's nations, upon seeing that their problems drove Veidt to murder millions, would forge an even more secure and lasting peace than otherwise.

And maybe Nite Owl will get "Abs of Steel." Seriously, I don't think I'm alone in guessing that things wouldn't work out like this. I mean, it's *possible* that the world could end up better off—and if it did, then telling the truth would be the moral choice. The problem is, however, that we can't know the results of actions beforehand. We can only say what we think would likely result. Revealing Veidt's plot, as discussed earlier, would most likely result in more harm than good overall.

Rorschach doesn't seem to fare any better under rule utilitarianism, because it's hard to have a rule established about such an unusual case. Rule utilitarians would generally recommend a rule of truth-telling, or at least a rule of not lying, because both lead to good consequences overall (although, like Kant, they would make a distinction between truth-telling and not lying). But the normal rules of truth-telling don't apply here: there is so much more at stake, and the situation so exceptional, that following a rule established on what generally happens when we lie seems too hasty and against the spirit of utilitarianism. Without some precedents or a reliable means of predicting the future, there's no way to establish a rule to apply in Rorschach's case, and then we fall back on act utilitarianism, and we know what that says—"Shut up, Walter!"

Judging Rorschach

For utilitarians, it is wrong to tell the truth in Rorschach's case if the most important moral consideration is the result of truth-telling (and the result is likely to be as expected). Kant is more ambiguous; he would say that Rorschach should exercise some practical reasoning or judgment. Since Rorschach isn't morally required to tell the truth, and the chance of world peace hangs in the balance, it would make a lot of sense if he just kept his mouth shut. For all their differences, Kant and the utilitarians are often not that far apart in their conclusions, and when this happens, the moral case for silence is even stronger. And Rorschach is the strong, silent type, isn't he? [12]

NOTES

1. *Watchmen*, chap. XII, p. 20.

2. Ibid.

3. It's unclear because Dr. Manhattan seems to perform his actions because they are determined by the physical laws of the universe, not because they should be done.

4. Immanuel Kant, *Grounding for the Metaphysics of Morals* (1785), trans. James W. Ellington (Indianapolis: Hackett, 1994), p. 429. (The pagination is standard for Kant's writings, and appear in most reputable editions.)

5. One way to avoid the conflict is just to not say anything—a duty not to lie does not imply a duty to tell the truth. But doing so may give away the person we are hiding just as easily as if we had simply told the murderer the person was hiding with us.

6. See his *On a Supposed Right to Lie for Philanthropic Concerns*, pp. 63–68, included in the edition of *Grounding for the Metaphysics of Morals* cited in note 4. Kant's position here is extreme, even for him, and has generated a huge literature; see Roger J. Sullivan, *Immanuel Kant's Moral Theory* (Cambridge, UK: Cambridge University Press, 1989), pp. 173–179, and Christine Korsgaard, "The Right to Lie: Kant on Dealing with Evil," in *Creating the Kingdom of Ends* (Cambridge, UK: Cambridge University Press, 1996), pp. 133–158.

7. This discussion is taken from Barbara Herman, "Moral Deliberation and the Derivation of Duties," in *The Practice of Moral Judgment* (Cambridge, MA: Harvard University Press, 1993), p. 156.

8. For more on this line of argument, see Korsgaard, *Creating the Kingdom of Ends*, p. 146. This argument helps explain why Batman does not kill the Joker, even though it would undoubtedly prevent many innocent deaths; see Mark D. White's "Why Doesn't Batman Kill the Joker?" in Mark D. White and Robert Arp, eds., *Batman and Philosophy* (Hoboken, NJ: Wiley, 2008), p. 12.

9. *Editor*—No there aren't.

10. See chapter 5 of this book, "Means, Ends, and the Critique of Pure Superheroes," by J. Robert Loftis, for more on utilitarianism.

11. Again, see the chapter by Rob Loftis in this book for more on act and rule utilitarianism.

12. Special thanks to Erik Henriksen and Vista Ritchie for their many helpful comments on this chapter.

PART THREE

THE METAPHYSICS OF
DR. MANHATTAN

DR. MANHATTAN,
I PRESUME?

James DiGiovanna

Am I Who I Am?

You go to sleep. You wake up. You have no doubt that you're the same person you were yesterday. You look the same, remember most of the same things, are mad at the same people, and owe money to the same bank. But what if you looked over your shoulder and saw another one of you? Or what if you were destroyed at the submolecular level by an "intrinsic field remover," and then you reconstituted your body just by thinking yourself into existence? Or what if you ceased to exist on Earth and suddenly appeared on Mars?

Most of us never have to worry about that sort of thing, but that's only because fewer than 5 percent of us are atomic-powered superheroes like Dr. Manhattan. And yet the questions about Dr. Manhattan's continued identity, whether he's the same person after he teleports or when he splits into three people and then rejoins into one or when he remembers the future and looks forward to the past, are all questions that

103

philosophers have raised about the *identity* of persons—not only because philosophers have nothing better to do with their time, but because these are questions that get at the heart of what it is for you to be you and not someone else.

The most basic question of identity is: how am I the same person when I undergo so many changes? My size, shape, thoughts, memories, personality, and preferences change over time. This is all nicely exaggerated in the case of Dr. Manhattan, who was originally a research scientist named Jon Osterman. One day, Osterman stepped into a piece of experimental equipment, the "intrinsic field" removing chamber, and he was disintegrated. A short time later, he reappeared, now colored blue and with unbelievable powers. Was this the same man who stepped into the machine originally? And in what way, specifically, was he the same, when virtually everything about him had changed?

Selves, Bundles, and Memories

The question of identity first appears in modern thought in the work of the philosopher René Descartes (1596–1650), who concluded that the one thing he could be certain of was his own existence: "I think therefore I exist."[1] But what sort of thing am I? Descartes said that people were "thinking things," that they were essentially nonmaterial minds. But sometimes we stop thinking, such as when we sleep. When we start again, how do we know that it's the same thinker doing the thinking? How can we be sure we exist across time?

Descartes didn't say much about the problem of sameness over time, but he did make an assumption that later philosophers doubted: beneath the ever-changing set of thoughts and perceptions—yet independent of them—lies a mind that is consistent across time, even as its content changes. In other words, Descartes didn't identify himself with his thoughts, but rather thought of himself as a being who produced or entertained those thoughts. So for him, to be is to *be* a thinker who *has* thoughts. Notably, Descartes thought that the mind could exist without the body, since thoughts are so very different from material things.

The philosopher David Hume (1711–1776) had different ideas on the subject. Of course there are thoughts, but Hume didn't see any reason to believe that there was a thinker distinct from those thoughts. He said that when he looked into his mind, he saw thoughts and perceptions but no self. He saw only "a bundle or collection of different perceptions."[2] If there were no perceptions, ideas, or content in our minds, according to Hume, we would cease to exist. So, reasoned Hume, there is no underlying self or mind or thinker—only thoughts. We imagine there is a self because those thoughts occur in sequence, with one thought giving rise to the next, and this chain of continuous thought is mistaken for a continuity of identity.

Now think of Dr. Manhattan's origin: he enters the "intrinsic field" test chamber and is completely disintegrated. And yet something remains, something that thinks, and remembers, and can reconstitute his body. If we follow Descartes, this thing would be the mind of Dr. Manhattan. If we follow Hume, it would just be a continuation of the thoughts Osterman was having before he was disintegrated. But the latter interpretation seems very odd here: how would this chain of thoughts continue if Osterman's body had disintegrated? Isn't a brain necessary to do the thinking? So maybe this shows that Descartes was right, and that there could be a disembodied mind of some sort. Or could the thoughts, all by themselves, just continue, and continue to be associated? This seems strange, but then, so does Jon Osterman's disintegration and reappearance as Dr. Manhattan!

Still, if the thoughts continued to be thought, and they hung together in some way, then that's roughly the same as saying that Dr. Manhattan existed as a disembodied mind.

One of the reasons that Hume didn't trust the idea of a mind that existed by itself was that no one had ever seen such a thing. No sensory evidence for it existed. All we have are bodies and collections of thoughts. If thought stopped, and the body was destroyed, what would maintain identity? But if it actually occurred, Dr. Manhattan's reappearance would be some evidence for the continued existence of a mind apart from a body. Still, what makes this Jon Osterman's mind and not some new mind? How do we know that by virtue of continuity, the being who appears in the research lab, now colored blue and glowing with power, is the same as the research scientist who was destroyed by the intrinsic field machine?

Hume's predecessor, the philosopher John Locke (1632–1704), had approached the problem by saying that our memories tie together our identities. If this is the case, then we remain the same people over time because we have a continuity in one area of thought: those things that we remember from a first-person perspective.[3] Dr. Manhattan can claim to be Jon Osterman because he remembers being Jon Osterman. Memory holds his identity together. But Hume thought that this wouldn't work, because our memories fade over time. If memory is the key to identity, then we must be different people now than we were ten years ago. In fact, tomorrow I will have forgotten most of the passing thoughts I had today. Does that mean I'm not the same person? For Hume, the troubling answer is "yes." We really do become different people, perhaps incrementally, but ultimately we have little in common with our earlier selves because the memories I have today and those I had ten years ago barely overlap. Even if I remembered everything that happened to me in the past, which is never the case, I'd still have a different set of memories in the future, since I'd have added many new ones. So my memory-self is never going to be the same.

But Dr. Manhattan doesn't have this problem. One of the most interesting features of the character is that he remembers both forward and backward in time. So not only does his future self have all of the memories of his past self, his past self has all of the memories of his future self, at least after he becomes Dr. Manhattan. We can assume that Jon Osterman had no such power, or he would have remembered not to leave his lab coat in the intrinsic field-removing machine! This may be why, in the final book of the series, Dr. Manhattan says of a trap that Ozymandias had laid for him, "It didn't kill Osterman. Did you think it would kill me?"[4] In other words, he sees himself as distinct from Osterman. Nonetheless, if memory is the basis of identity, then the problem of continuity of identity over time is solved for Dr. Manhattan, assuming that Dr. Manhattan is distinct from Osterman.

But Dr. Manhattan makes it clear that for the rest of us, the problem remains. Unlike Dr. Manhattan, we forget parts of our pasts and acquire new memories in the future. If memory is identity, then our identities must be subject to change. But no matter what I forget, in many ways I'm still myself over time: I'm still guilty of past crimes, liable for future debts, and legally responsible for contracts I signed in the past. So, then, what is it that secures my identity over time?

I Am Not My Body

Derek Parfit, the leading contemporary philosopher on the question of identity over time, often uses science fiction examples to illustrate his points. Parfit would probably love Dr. Manhattan, because the character raises many of the same questions that the philosopher does.

One of Parfit's most famous examples is what he calls "the teletransporter," similar to the transporters on *Star Trek*.[5] This machine scans a human body, destroying it as it records the position of every atom, and then sends the information to another machine on Mars, where the body is perfectly recreated. Since it's safe to assume that psychological content is carried by the atoms that make up the human brain, all of the person's memories, thoughts, intentions, beliefs, desires, and personal dispositions are preserved in the being that emerges on Mars. But is it the same person?

This question fits very neatly with *Watchmen*, in which Dr. Manhattan teleports himself and Laurie Juspeczyk to Mars. Are they the same persons after the teleportation? Or are they merely replicas, perfect copies of the originals recreated on Mars? What about Jon Osterman before he walked into the intrinsic field-removing machine and the Dr. Manhattan who emerged later: are they the same, or is Dr. Manhattan merely an imperfect replica of Jon Osterman? Is the blue coloring of his skin a copy error? Where is the original? And what would constitute an absolute test to see whether someone was the same person as some previous person?

To answer this last question, Parfit reviewed the history of ideas on personal identity and came up with a number of categories to describe the various positions. First, there's what he called "the physical criterion," which states that a person is the same person if some significant part of his or her material body (specifically, the brain) continues to exist and traces a "physically continuous spatio-temporal path"—in other words, a line through space and time.[6] For example, as you stand still, you trace an unbroken path through time from the recent past to the present. If you move, you trace a path through space as well. Plotting both the path through space and the path through time, you could show an unbroken "spatio-temporal path."

Now look at Dr. Manhattan. He enters the intrinsic field-removing chamber, and he is disintegrated. And then, some time later, bits of him start to appear, briefly, in the research facility: a nervous system, a circulatory system, musculature, and so on. Then, finally, he rebuilds himself entirely, although he's clearly changed. The matter he's composed of is probably not the same matter he was made of before (it's considerably more blue, for example). So there's no reason to believe that his physical self traces a continuous path through space-time. It seems, rather, that as a material being, he ceased to exist. So, can we say he's the same person? If we accept the physical criterion, we cannot, and so identity becomes a problem.

But surely that doesn't affect an ordinary person, does it? Unfortunately, yes, it does, because what happened to Dr. Manhattan happens to all of us, only a little more slowly. Most of the cells in our bodies will die and be replaced many times during our lives. We'll take in and excrete great amounts of matter, transforming ourselves almost entirely. So, in a sense, none of us traces a continuous path through space-time, at least if we focus only on our material bodies. But Parfit notes that the physical criterion doesn't require that the whole body be preserved; for the most part, people who accept the physical criterion think that only the brain needs to be preserved. This, one assumes, is because the brain isn't just a lump of physical matter like any other—it houses or creates our psychological states.

If I'm My Mind, How Many of Me Are There?

So, maybe what matters is not our matter, but our minds. This is the position of philosophers who hold what Parfit calls "the psychological criterion." According to the psychological criterion, what matters for personal identity is that we have some continuity in purely mental terms—having the same memories, beliefs, desires, and dispositions to behave in certain ways, or at least some significant percentage of the same memories, beliefs, desires, and dispositions. This would connect Dr. Manhattan, at the moment he reappears, with Jon Osterman, the man he was before the accident. Even though Osterman apparently ceased to exist for a time, when Dr. Manhattan appeared he had all of Osterman's memories and personality. He was still emotionally connected to his girlfriend, he still was interested in research in physics, he continued to behave roughly as he had before. Of course, over time this changed, but that's true for all people. Still, when Dr. Manhattan appeared, he had most of Osterman's psychological content, and he had it from the same first-person perspective that Osterman had it. In other words, he saw the world through the eyes of Osterman, and that, it seems, is possible only for someone who is or was Osterman.

So Dr. Manhattan has the psychological continuity needed for his identity to be clearly that of Osterman. Dr. Manhattan also says something that indicates that he had that psychological continuity even when he didn't have a body: he tells Ozymandias that "restructuring myself after the subtraction of my intrinsic field was the first trick I learned."[7] In other words, Dr. Manhattan figured out how to rebuild his body when he had no body. In order to learn something, he must have had some sort of psychological existence. Dr. Manhattan, it seems, has psychological continuity without the need for physical continuity. There are two ways to think of this psychological continuity: either it could be something like Descartes' idea of the mind, a simple, indivisible substance that thinks and is not *reducible* to anything else. Or, the psychological self might be, as Hume thought, reducible to its contents—if we completely describe the mind's contents, the thoughts, memories, dispositions, and all other psychological facts, we'll have completely described the self. In other words, the self is only the psychological content; it's not something in addition to that content, as Descartes thought.

But that raises an interesting question: what if, instead of one Dr. Manhattan appearing, two had? In other words, if Dr. Manhattan is a mind in the way Descartes thought, then replicating him would produce only a replica: the real Dr. Manhattan would be distinct. If the psychological continuity, however, is not a simple thing, but instead a bundle of beliefs and desires and memories, as Hume thought, then it's possible that its replication would not be another thing, but would be indistinguishable on all levels from the original. For example, if you had a signed first edition of James Joyce's *Ulysses*, then a photocopy of it would not be the same thing as the original. In a sense, the signed first edition is not reducible to its contents, the words on the page. Because of the special nature of that particular book, it's important to have the original. But if you had a computer file with the text of *Ulysses*, copying the file to another hard drive wouldn't give you a lesser something, a mere copy. It would give you the exact same thing you had in the first place.

If you download an MP3 to your computer, however, and then copy it to your iPod, the one on your iPod and the one on your hard drive are two separate things, but not in the sense of an original and a copy. They're both the same, neither one more original or truer than the other. So, if Dr. Manhattan is reducible to his psychological content, then, like an MP3, he's merely data: his thoughts, beliefs, intentions, desires, and so on. If we duplicate those, is there a sense in which there is an "original"? When Dr. Manhattan has no body, he's just thoughts, or just data. He's like that MP3 file: it doesn't matter where you have it, it's the same data.

So imagine that instead of one Dr. Manhattan, two had appeared after the intrinsic field accident, each having the memories and the personality of Jon Osterman. Which one would be the original? There's really no way to say, since Osterman's body was destroyed, and there's no clear path through time and space that can be traced out for the original being. When he was disembodied, he existed only as thoughts, and a copy of those thoughts is exactly the same as the original.

This isn't idle speculation, either in the comic book world of *Watchmen* or in the real world. At one point in the book, Dr. Manhattan actually splits himself into three separate entities. They seem to be able to function independently of one another: one of his selves talks to Laurie Juspeczyk, while another repairs a broken glass tumbler.[8] If Dr. Manhattan's identity was like that of Descartes' conception of the mind, he would have to be a single self. But here, he's three selves, with three first-person points of view. It seems completely contrary to the idea of a self that it include simultaneous and distinct points of view and simultaneous and distinct subjective experiences. And later, Dr. Manhattan merges back into a single self. Was he three selves for a time and then a single self later, or must we think of him as becoming a new self with each split and re-fusion?

Although few of us will gain Dr. Manhattan–like superpowers, there are nonetheless real-world instances of people splitting in two, at least in a limited sense, and these raise very serious questions about the nature of personal identity. The contemporary philosopher Thomas Nagel addresses this in his essay "Brain Bisection and the Unity of Consciousness," in which he discusses a kind of surgery that has been performed many times: cutting the corpus callosum, a neural bridge between the two hemispheres of the brain.[9] In the past, the entire corpus callosum was sometimes cut to treat severe epilepsy. With the two hemispheres of the brain separated, information does not easily pass between them. In one experiment, an image of an object was shown to a patient's left eye, which connects to the right hemisphere of the brain. The patient was then asked to find, by touch, the item he had seen from a group of items. He correctly chose the object. But then the patient was asked what the item was, and he could not say.[10] The left hemisphere of the brain controls language, and it had not received information about the object. What seemed to occur was that two consciousnesses now inhabited one body.

So, not unlike the case of Dr. Manhattan, an ordinary person can indeed be split in two. Since the two halves of the brain are continuous, psychologically, with at least part of the person from before the surgery, it seems that one person has become two, and the psychological criterion for identity (continuity of memories, beliefs, desires, and so on) can't be used to pick out a unique individual who is continuous over time. Furthermore, it is at least theoretically possible that the two halves of the brain could be transplanted into different bodies.[11] Assume that there is a person who is perfectly equal in the distribution of abilities across the hemispheres. Imagine that this person's brain is split in two, and each half is transplanted into a different body.[12] Which of the two new people has the same identity as the old one? There seems to be no way to tell. If they both are the original person, then we have the odd situation where a person could get into an argument with himself, kill himself, and walk away from the murder unharmed. Or if neither is the original person, then that person must be, in a sense, dead, but his thoughts, dreams, intentions, and desires live on in the two other people. How could that be possible?

Superheroes and Super-Identity

Clearly, the concept of an "individual" or a "person" becomes very difficult at this point, as it does in the case of Dr. Manhattan and his split selves. But it's possible, in Dr. Manhattan's case, that he experiences all of those selves simultaneously, that his superpowered consciousness actually encompasses more than one subjective point of view. In other words, even if in splitting he creates replicas, maybe he exists as all these replicas at once, his superconsciousness taking in all of their points of view, controlling all of their actions, and truly being them. But for an ordinary human, this seems impossible. If I were to be split in two, it would be very hard for anyone to say whether I was alive or dead, or whether one or the other of the new people created from my brain is me. Surely, it couldn't be that both of those people are me, because their experiences are now distinct from each other. They no longer share a unified consciousness, and if someone has a point of view different from mine, it's pretty much given that this person is not me. So the problem of personal identity arises again.

In fact, Dr. Manhattan may be the only being who truly has identity. We would be hard-pressed to say whether we continue to exist after teleporting or after having our brains split, and this raises serious questions even about our everyday notions of identity. But Dr. Manhattan's consciousness is not tied to his body; if he teleports, he remains the same, even if all of his matter changes, because he can exist without matter. And he can split into two or three and still retain his identity by having simultaneous consciousness in different bodies. But most important, if we are ourselves because of the continuity of our memories, then we cease to be ourselves as we age and forget things. But Dr. Manhattan, by remembering both forward and backward in time, doesn't have this problem. This means that Dr. Manhattan has one superpower that no one else has: he can overcome the philosophical problem of identity!

NOTES

1. In chapter 4 of Descartes' *Discourse on Method* (1637), available online at www .literature.org/authors/descartes-rene/reason-discourse/chapter-04.html.

2. In Book 1, section 6, of Hume's *Treatise of Human Nature* (1739), available in a number of editions.

3. Chapter 27, section 16, of Locke's *Enquiries Concerning Human Understanding* (1748), also available in various editions.

4. *Watchmen*, chap. XII, p. 18.

5. See Parfit's *Reasons and Persons* (Oxford, UK: Oxford University Press, 1984), p. 199.

6. Ibid., p. 203.

7. *Watchmen*, chap. XII, p. 18.

8. Ibid., chap. III, p. 5.

9. In Nagel's *Mortal Questions* (Cambridge, UK: Cambridge University Press, 1979), pp. 147–164.

10. Ibid., p. 152.

11. This idea occurs first in David Wiggins, *Identity and Spatio-Temporal Continuity* (Oxford, UK: Basil Blackwell, 1967), p. 50, cited in Parfit, *Reasons and Persons*, p. 254.

12. There's an additional impossibility here because some parts of the brain are not neatly divided into the two hemispheres, but rather exist beneath the two hemispheres; we'll assume that this problem can be overcome.

A TIMELY ENCOUNTER: DR. MANHATTAN AND HENRI BERGSON

Christopher M. Drohan

For Dr. Manhattan, time is out of joint. Past, present, and future seem to blend together. In fact, though, his concept of time bears a remarkable similarity to that of the philosopher Henri Bergson (1859–1941), who showed that the common notion of linear time is fraught with problems that modern science and philosophy must contend with.

"His watch isn't the only thing that's broken."

When Dr. Manhattan's breakup plunges him into depression and nostalgia, he teleports himself to an abandoned bar somewhere in the middle of the Arizona desert, where he met his girlfriend, Janey. Finding a well-worn photo of Janey and himself still on the bar wall, Manhattan remembers Christmas 1959, when Janey gave him a gold ring. In this memory, he tells her that he'll always want her, although in the same moment he admits to himself that he's lying, for he can actually "hear her shouting at me in 1963; sobbing in 1966" as he falls in love with another woman and leaves Janey, respectively.[1] Suddenly, we become aware that Manhattan somehow has the power to predict or even see the future. Shortly after this incident, Manhattan remarks to Janey one night that sometimes he feels as if he's "been here all the time."[2] We begin to wonder whether he has a similar ability to see the past, too, although the way in which Manhattan says it makes it seem as if he's still not quite sure of things himself.

Jumping forward in time now to 1985, while Manhattan is escorting his new girlfriend, Laurie, around his Martian palace, he finally begins to reveal his vision of time. He tells her, "Everything is preordained. Even my responses. . . . We're all puppets, Laurie. I'm just a puppet who can see the strings."[3] Manhattan follows this up by telling Laurie exactly how their argument is going to unfold, saying it's all part of the "destiny of the world" and that "There is no future. There is no past. Do you see? Time is simultaneous, an intricately structured jewel that humans insist on viewing one edge at a time, when the whole design is visible in every facet."[4] Accordingly, Manhattan doesn't see the point in debating the future, as he somehow already knows how it's going to unfold, and feels that all of it is meaningless.

We must question, though, in what sense Manhattan "sees" this future, and likewise how he recalls the past. Given his superhuman intelligence, it's no wonder that Manhattan has an overwhelming grasp of time in all of its senses and tenses. On the one hand, his ability to manipulate matter at an atomic level means that he is similarly conscious of that material scale. Furthermore, he seems noticeably aware of events unfolding on the other side of the planet.[5] On top of this, Manhattan has the incredible ability to recall the past, as evidenced by the vivid sequences of flashbacks he keeps having. In fact, he claims that he can even see "the ancient spectacle that birthed the rubble" of the universe.[6] At the very least, then, Manhattan is privy to a spectacle of time greater than the sum of all human minds, a spectacle beside which all "human life is brief and mundane."[7]

And yet even as Manhattan says these words, we cannot help but feel his hypocrisy. Why, if everything is so pointless, has he carried on with his human relationships until now? When Laurie challenges his vision of the future and asks him to tell her how things end, he can only say that "the details are vague" and that "there's some sort of static obscuring the future, preventing any clear impression."[8] Why, if everything is ultimately determined, does he have such a hard time predicting how it will unfold? When he offers the excuse that some sort of "electromagnetic pulse of a mass warhead detonation" might conceivably cause this vagueness, we nonetheless feel as if he's not so certain of his own destiny, and that his vision of the future might just be skewed.[9]

Bergson Saves Manhattan

The philosopher Henri Bergson (1859–1941) offers a unique conception of knowledge that can help us make sense of Dr. Manhattan's experience of time. Bergson argued that despite whatever perceptions we have, our bodies are continually acting and reacting to the world independently of these perceptions. For example, we don't need to imagine every step in order to walk. Nor do we have to think about our hearts beating for them to keep on pumping. The fact is that our bodies are equipped with all sorts of "instincts" that react either before or with our mental impressions of physical contact. Accordingly, Bergson doesn't see the brain as a sort of magical apparatus by which physical encounters with the body are transformed into mental sensations. Rather, the mental images are mere addendums to a much more complex series of physical actions and reactions, a much broader kind of "perception" that involves both body and mind.[10]

Accordingly, knowledge is not a matter of accurately representing our perceptions. Instead, knowledge consists of our ability *to act* in the world. The value of our mental images comes from the way in which they organize our different perceptions according to their use-value. This in turn necessitates that we have powerful memories that can conjure up images of how objects *were* used so that we can perceive how they can be used again.[11] In this way, every perception is "merely an occasion for remembering" for we "measure in practice the degree of [a percept's] reality by [its] degree of utility."[12] In other words, we perceive most clearly that which we know how to use. Perception is therefore a function of our actions in the world, which in turn rely on memory.[13]

Dr. Manhattan is a poignant example of this principle. Try as he might to realize an objective scientific image of the universe, his notion is polluted with images of events from his past. This leads him to the profound realization that every one of our ideas is hopelessly entwined with our past experiences, and that the whole of our past persists in even the simplest of thoughts. For example, after telling Laurie that all of time is simultaneous, he reminds her that even her earliest memory "isn't gone," that it's "still here," and she only has to "let [herself] see it."[14] These few words are enough to bring back a very vivid image of Laurie's past for her, while it reminds us that even though we don't walk around with images of our entire past suspended before our minds, somehow they're always there alongside us.

Bergson was quick to point out that all "perceptions are undoubtedly interlaced with memories," and inversely, memories only become "actual by borrowing the body of some perception," some present image of the past.[15] The "profound" mistake of some philosophers, however, is to conclude from this fact that there is only a difference of degree between memories and perceptions, and that memories are a form of "weakened perception," whose truth value is dubious.[16] Bergson instead argued that the difference between memory and perception is actually a difference in *kind*.

Active vs. Passive Time

The key to unraveling the difference between perception and memory lies in the difference between "voluntary" and "involuntary" memory. *Voluntary* memory "records, in the form of memory-images, all the events of our daily life as they occur in time" and "neglects no detail." In this way, voluntary memory is a "representation," a mental image of our past. *Involuntary* memory, on the other hand, is more like the memory of a "lesson I have learned." For example, we recall the involuntary memory of learning to ride a bicycle every time we hop on and start riding one. We don't need to picture the act in order to do it; rather, it comes naturally, so much so that we might even believe it was "innate," were we not able to voluntarily conjure up the memory-image of having learned to ride it.[17] Thus, the difference (in kind) between voluntary and involuntary memories is that the former are perceived, while the latter are acted out in concrete "movements."[18]

In that all of our memory-images are imagined presently, while all of our actions precede these images, Bergson noted that there is a second difference in kind between voluntary and involuntary memory. Actions belong to the "pure past" that precedes all of our perceptions, while "every *attentive* perception" is actually "a *reflection*" on this pure past.[19] In this way, there really is no difference between present images and recalled ones, as they are both memories of materials and objects that *were*. Even if we are looking at something right in front of us, the fact that this image has duration means that its image is a mix of past and present images. Psychological and scientific experiments have shown that such "afterimages" interfere with our perception of objects even while they are before our very eyes. This is to say that past memories are so mixed up with our present sensations that it's impossible to differentiate the two.[20] Perhaps this is why Manhattan suffers from so many flashbacks—his ingenious mind is so hyperaware that it realizes afterimages as distinct images.

In our image of time, the past, the present, and even the future are all simultaneously "present" to perception, as "every perception is already memory."[21] We are reminded of the words of Plato (c. 428–347 BCE) in *Timaeus*: "We say . . . it *was* and *shall be*, but on a true reckoning we should only say *is*, reserving *was* and *shall be* for the process of change in time."[22] The past is a matter of *actions* that take place before we can imagine them. In this way, all of our "ideas" are "pure recollections summoned from the depths of memory" that emerge as "memory-images" that are "more and more capable of inserting themselves into the motor diagram" of our bodies, which is to say, into actual *movements*.[23]

Thus, to sum everything up, as we go about our lives, we are constantly shifting between the *image* and the *act* of reality. Memory-images and imaginary ideas continually fold back upon the actions and the habits that cause them, as we oscillate between *perception* and the *pure past*.[24]

Manhattan Standard Time

Now let's turn back to Dr. Manhattan to see how Bergson's ideas can help us understand his predicament, and how their two theories of time begin to converge. Manhattan comes close to the Bergsonian concept of time when he says things like, "Perhaps the world is not made. Perhaps nothing is made. Perhaps it simply is, has been, will always be there. . . . A clock without a craftsman."[25] Bergson would interpret this as a different way of stating his idea that at the level of the pure past, all things act upon and react to one another in an unbroken continuity. Where we imagine causes and effects, there is nothing but pure and uninterrupted movements, a "fluidity" of matter that the intellect then breaks up into "discontinuous" images.[26] As *Watchmen* proceeds, Manhattan appears to be getting closer to this fluidity and toward an intuition of the pure and infinite past.

Consider Manhattan's final words to Ozymandias: "'In the end?' Nothing ends, Adrian. Nothing ever ends."[27] Comments like these show us that Manhattan, like Bergson before him, has a concept of the pure past that continues to shape our present images of the world and our actions in it. The more that Dr. Manhattan tries to make sense of this pure past, the more he finds that his ideas of it fail to grasp it, for they differ in kind from this infinite and active realm. When he acknowledges certain "thermo-dynamic miracles . . . events with odds against so astronomical they're effectively impossible," and that life is one such miracle, he has stumbled upon Bergson's idea that every living act is miraculous, in that through our acts we enter into the infinite and continuous motion of the universe, which is "effectively impossible" to capture in a complete image of thought.[28] In fact, "the world is so full of people, so crowded with these miracles that they become commonplace and we forget . . . I forget. We gaze continually at the world and it grows dull in our perceptions. Yet seen from another's vantage point, as if new, it may still take the breath away. Come . . . dry your eyes, for you are life, rarer than a quark and unpredictable beyond the dreams of Heisenberg; the clay in which the forces that shape all things leave their fingerprints most clearly."[29] In this passage, Manhattan gives a name to his intuition of time's purity and infinity, calling it "life."

For Bergson, as for Manhattan, time is nothing like a clock, a calendar, or any other linear measurement. Time is *duration*, a lived experience that is "essentially memory, consciousness and freedom." As we live our lives, our present experience is a "pure becoming" of ourselves in time, which is therefore "always outside itself," as our image of the present always already expresses a moment of time that has passed. One must ask oneself, "How would a new present come about if the old present did not pass at the same time that it *is* present? How would any present whatsoever pass, if it were not past *at the same time* as present?" Thus, "the past is 'contemporaneous' with the present that it *has* been."[30]

Accordingly, Bergson distinguished a difference in kind between our memory-images of time and the pure past from which they are drawn. That our bodies continually act without thinking, that we never forget how to breathe, how to walk, or how to conduct ourselves in every which way, shows the perpetual influence of our pure past. And that we can recall, at any moment, images and ideas that we identify with the past shows that we have access to this virtual past, which is like an infinite memory bank existing alongside all of our thoughts from which all of our memory-images are drawn. With every living act, we "leap" intuitively into this pure past and extract new images from it.[31] Thus, we move "from the past to the present," and not vice versa, as the present is a mere "translation" and expansion of this free past into a determined and significant image form.[32] "Everything happens as if the universe were a tremendous Memory," a "monism of Time" of which we get these warped pictures.[33]

Everyday Time Travel

By the end of *Watchmen*, Manhattan is living this "monism of Time." Perhaps he has been helped along by the tachyon field emanating from Ozymandias's lair. Tachyon particles travel "backwards in time," and it seems that Manhattan is able to seize on their power so that he's not only aware of, but acting in, multiple temporalities simultaneously.[34] It's as if he's somehow managed to tap into pure time itself, in such a way as to be able to operate independently of its images.

As strange as this may seem, Bergson's philosophy of time reminds us that we are all capable of making the same kind of leaps through time, because our living actions and memories show that we are in perpetual contact with the past. In our own way, we're all Dr. Manhattans, caught somewhere between the past and the present, struggling to carve out those actions and thoughts that will be our future. For the future is as much an image of thought as the past is, and likewise the pure future arrives before our image of it, just as the pure past does. Bergson's philosophy and Manhattan's intuitions therefore call into question the "progress" of time itself, for no matter what our image of time is, time's truth resides in infinite and eternal actions, which will always exceed our notions of them. Ironically, the truth of time resides in its timelessness, a constant state of moving and becoming without end, as alive and free as all the creatures that partake in it.

NOTES

1. *Watchmen*, chap. IV, p. 11.

2. Ibid., p. 13.

3. Ibid., chap. IX, p. 5.

4. Ibid., p. 6.

5. For instance, he is able to monitor political events in Afghanistan without having to go there. See ibid., chap. III, p. 13.

6. Ibid., chap. IX, p. 17.

7. Ibid.

8. Ibid.

9. Ibid.

10. Henri Bergson, *Matter and Memory*, trans. N. M. Paul and W. S. Palmer (New York: Zone Books, 1991), p. 34.

11. Ibid., pp. 37–38.

12. Ibid., p. 66.

13. Ibid., p. 67.

14. *Watchmen*, chap. XI, p. 6.

15. Bergson, *Matter and Memory*, p. 67.

16. Ibid., p. 68.

17. Ibid., pp. 80–81.

18. Ibid., pp. 90–91.

19. Ibid., p. 102.

20. Ibid., p. 133.

21. Ibid., p. 150.

22. Plato, *Timaeus and Critias*, trans. Desmond Lee (London: Penguin Classics, 1971), p. 51.

23. Bergson, *Matter and Memory*, p. 125.

24. Ibid., pp. 151–167.

25. *Watchmen*, chap. IV, p. 28.

26. Henri Bergson, *Creative Evolution*, trans. Arthur Mitchell (New York: Barnes and Noble, 2005), p. 102.

27. *Watchmen*, chap. XII, p. 27.

28. Ibid., chap. IX, p. 26.

29. Ibid., pp. 27–28. Werner Heisenberg's (1901–1976) theory was that the closer we come to locating the actual position of an atomic particle, the less we can ascertain about its momentum. Bergson had already made this point many years before him, although in philosophical form. For Bergson, the closer we get to an image of an object in space and time, the further we are from the reality that this image is actually only a small part of the infinite and continuous flow of universal matter.

30. Gilles Deleuze, *Bergsonism*, trans. Hugh Tomlinson (New York: Zone Books, 1991), pp. 55–58.

31. Ibid., p. 56.

32. Ibid., p. 63.

33. Ibid., pp. 77–78.

34. *Watchmen*, chap. XII, p. 8.

FREE WILL AND FOREKNOWLEDGE: DOES JON REALLY KNOW WHAT LAURIE WILL DO NEXT, AND CAN SHE DO OTHERWISE?

Arthur Ward

He's Got Foreknowledge, and He's Not Afraid to Use It

Dr. Jon Osterman is big, blue, and naked—and he can kill you just by wishing you dead. So if he orders you to do something, you would be wise to do it! That's just commonsense. But here is an even more disturbing scenario: what if he tells you, just as a matter of fact, that you *will* do something? Suppose he tells you, as he tells Laurie Juspeczyk, the Silk Spectre, at one point in *Watchmen*, that you will walk up the stairs to have a conversation with him.[1] It will no doubt occur to you, as it does to Laurie: what if you don't walk upstairs? Couldn't you prove him wrong by doing otherwise? In the story, we don't get a chance to find out because Laurie *does* walk upstairs to have a conversation with him. Yet it seems that if Jon really knew without a doubt that Laurie would walk upstairs, there is only one possible thing Laurie could have done: *walk upstairs*. If so, the disturbing conclusion would be that Laurie had no other option. Her fate was predetermined. Does this mean that Jon's foreknowledge rules out the possibility of free will?

This puzzle is not new to philosophers. Jon's big blue nakedness may be an unusual twist, but the problem of reconciling human free will with the presence of an all-knowing being (such as God) is a centuries-old question. This problem has been called *fatalism* (as in "fate," not "fatal"). So, to figure out whether Jon's foreknowledge rules out the possibility of free will, we'll consult some great minds of the past to see how they responded to fatalism.

Alternatives, Shmalternatives

Jon claims to have infallible foreknowledge of future events, and he also believes in *fatalism*, the theory that everything is predetermined or preordained. The reason that fatalism is so disturbing is that free will seems to require choosing between alternative possibilities. If you discover that all of your actions have been controlled by an evil scientist with a remote device, and that he's fooled you into thinking that you were controlling your own actions, would you think your actions were free? Probably not, since at any given moment there was nothing else you *could* have done. "But," you may say, "this example doesn't apply to the real world because in this example I'm being controlled by the evil scientist. And surely, in the real world, God is not controlling my every action, right?" Quite right.

So, now think of another case, where no one is controlling you, but there is still only a single path, a single set of actions, that you can take. Assume that there are no alternative possibilities open to you: your actions are predetermined. Do you have free will now? Philosophers disagree on this point. Some philosophers call themselves *compatibilists* about free will and believe that even without alternative possibilities, one can have free will if one *believes* that there are alternative possibilities. Other philosophers call themselves *incompatibilists*, arguing that without alternative possibilities, the "ability to do otherwise," free will is an illusion. If fatalism is correct, it rules out alternative possibilities, so that will be our concern here. The elimination of alternative possibilities is deeply disturbing to Laurie (and to you, I bet!), so we'll take that to be a significant threat to free will. Even if there are fancy compatibilist arguments out there, there isn't time to run through all of them in this chapter.

God, I Hope It's Not Fatal

It is central to many religious traditions that God is by definition all-powerful (*omnipotent*), perfectly good (*omnibenevolent*), and all-knowing (*omniscient*). It is also central to these traditions that God gave humans free will, thus explaining our capacity to commit sin and experience redemption. An age-old puzzle for the philosophy of religion is that our free will seems possibly inconsistent with God's omniscience. If God is omniscient, God knows *everything* and this knowledge is *infallible*. Suppose God knows infallibly that tomorrow at 8 p.m., you will sit in your favorite chair and read *Watchmen*. When 8 p.m. comes around, do you have any other option *but* to sit in your favorite chair and read *Watchmen*? If you choose *not* to sit in your favorite chair and read *Watchmen*, God would be wrong, and hence not omniscient. According to the previous definition, God *is* omniscient, and that seems to mean only one thing: if God knows that you will sit in your favorite chair and read *Watchmen* tomorrow at 8 p.m., you *will* do it.

Some philosophers have supposed that this means that come 8 p.m., you do not truly have the freedom to choose your activity, that your action is predetermined. You may *think* you have a choice between alternative actions, but this is merely an illusion. Note that no one is claiming that God is *forcing* you to sit in your favorite chair and read *Watchmen*, so it's not like the evil scientist example. The key point is just that God's foreknowledge seems to rule out alternative possibilities.

The way the problem of *theological* fatalism—the conflict between divine foreknowledge and human free will—has been explained thus far, it boils down to the fact that it's impossible to change or affect the past. When 8 p.m. rolls around, God already knew, in the past, what you would do. Since God's knowledge *then* was about the future, the infallibility of God's knowledge determined with certainty that you will sit in your favorite chair and read *Watchmen*.

A popular and ingenious solution to theological fatalism has been to take God's perspective out of time. The Christian philosophers Boethius (480–525) and St. Thomas Aquinas (1225–1274) both urged this solution to the problem.[2] You see, if God exists outside of time, God's knowledge is not tied to any particular date. Thus, the power to make free choices does not involve affecting the past. You can do whatever you choose to do, and God, from a timeless perspective, will know your choice. It is as if we are all characters in a movie, and God is able to unwind the movie reel and view all of the frames at once. Just because God can see everything does not mean that anyone's free will is constrained, or so the argument goes.

But timelessness alone does not rule out fatalism. Remember that Jon claims his perspective is timeless, yet he believes everything is a matter of fate. A movie reel, after all, always turns out the same way in the end. To retain alternative possibilities and reject fatalism, one should instead imagine God to be looking at a movie reel that branches off in countless different directions, each tracking the consequences of a possible choice you make. You get to choose which branch to follow, so it's not determined ahead of time. God's knowledge encompasses not only the actual decisions you make, but the possible decisions you *could* have made. This would reject the idea of fate and embrace the idea that we can control our future to some extent (with God just acting as scorekeeper).

Like most great philosophical puzzles, people are still arguing over this one. Some think that taking God out of time solves the problem, but others think that if it is impossible to affect the past, why think that it's any more plausible to affect timelessness?[3] Does a timeless branching movie reel even make sense? Sadly, we won't solve the problem here.

The solution to theological fatalism that we just discussed combines God's timelessness with a picture of God's knowledge that allows for alternative possibilities (the branching movie reel). When it comes to facing the problem of free will and foreknowledge in *Watchmen*, this second half of the solution isn't available to save the day. Jon insists, after all, that everything is "preordained." By this, he doesn't mean to reference God—he tells his girlfriend, Janey, that he doesn't think there *is* a God.[4] Rather, he means that the future is determined entirely by past events and is on a singular path, unable to be altered in any way (like a standard, nonbranching movie reel). If this were true, any given choice you are to make would be set in stone: there would be no alternative possibilities. But as we compare the problem of God's foreknowledge with Jon's foreknowledge, it's worth noting that Moore is deliberately setting the two side by side for comparison.

The Naked Watchmaker

As we saw, Jon does not think there is a God. He adds, "If there is, I'm not him." Yet throughout *Watchmen*, the reader is bombarded with constant reminders of Jon's godliness. One elegant symbol in the story is a watch. The title,

Watchmen, obviously refers in part to the roles of the various heroes and antiheroes as guardians, but Jon is a "watch-man" in a league of his own, and in three different respects. First, he has almost God-like foreknowledge (exactly *how* God-like is at issue in this chapter), so he is a watchman in the sense of being an observer. Second, the watch is a symbol for the inevitability of time's steady progress (note that the twelve chapters of the book count down the twelve hours of a clock). The gears of a watch move in a predictable pattern, admitting of no error or exception to its timekeeping. This is how Jon understands time: as an inevitable and deterministic series of predictable events, and he is the lone witness to its marvel. Finally, and most important to Jon's status as a demigod, is the centuries-old metaphor of God as a watchmaker.

The philosopher William Paley (1743–1805) is famous for comparing the human design of a pocket watch to God's design of the universe. He begins his book *Natural Theology* with the following argument: If one came across a pocket watch in the forest, one would observe the tight casing and the perfect harmony of the gears and conclude that rather than being a product of chance, the watch must have had a designer.[5] Similarly, when one observes the perfect rotation of the planets, for example, or the intricate and delicate machinery of a human body, the reasonable conclusion (according to Paley) is that it was the work of a designer, rather than a product of chance. Paley's argument is sometimes called the "argument from design" or "the teleological argument." The fact that Jon grew up as the son of a watchmaker (another watch-man) and creates his vast Martian palace in the form of a giant watch is therefore significant. He is settling into his metaphorical role as Paley's God-like designer: as the red glass palace emerges from the Martian sands, Jon asks, "Who makes the world?" and as he leaves this galaxy says, "For one less complicated," he thinks perhaps he'll create some human life.[6]

The World According to Big Blue

In chapter IV we see Jon sulking on Mars, remembering the incident in which he gained his power. As the chapter progresses, however, it seems less like he is *remembering* the past and more like he is *experiencing* it. The reader comes to understand that he sees time as an artificial construct that limits human perception. As he says to Laurie in his Martian palace, "Time is simultaneous, an intricately structured jewel that humans insist on viewing one edge at a time, when the whole design is visible in every facet."[7] By saying this, Jon is laying claim to timeless (even infallible) foreknowledge.

As we've seen, Jon also claims that fatalism is true. In chapter IV we see him tell his girlfriend Janey, "I can't prevent the future, to me it's already happening."[8] If both claims are true, it is bad news for free will. As Jon says, "We're all puppets, Laurie. I'm just one who can see the strings."[9] Let's go back to the movie-reel analogy for a moment. Remember, if one imagines God as seeing an unwound movie reel that branches off in every possible direction each time someone utilizes his or her free will, then God's timeless perspective doesn't mean that everyone's fate is determined. If Jon is correct, time is like a *conventional* movie reel, with a beginning, a middle, and an end, without any branching. No alternatives are possible—just fate. The good news for everyone is that given events that happen in the story, it's impossible for both of Jon's claims to be true. And as long as one claim can be rejected, either the timeless foreknowledge claim or the fatalism claim, it's still possible for Laurie to have free will in *Watchmen*. Let's consider the evidence from the text.

Why Jon Is Wrong

Several aspects of Jon Osterman's purported abilities do not quite add up. In chapter IX, how can he be surprised that Laurie is sleeping with Dan Dreiberg (Nite Owl) when he admitted to knowing it ahead of time? Why was he surprised in chapter III when the press told him his acquaintances were getting cancer? What does he mean in chapter I when he *thinks* he's close to discovering a gluino? These examples are totally inconsistent with his supposed foresight. Comic book and science fiction fans have two options when they come across such inconsistencies: they can criticize the author of the story as sloppy and unsophisticated, or they can more charitably imagine their own intricate explanations that iron out any wrinkles in the story. The uncharitable interpretation of the inconsistencies of Jon's powers in *Watchmen* is that Alan Moore doesn't know what the heck he's talking about when it comes to the philosophical puzzle of free will, foreknowledge, and fate, and that he's written a character that's logically impossible. But since most of what we know about Jon's powers of foresight is from Jon's own lips, it seems most fitting to believe that Jon himself is incorrect about the extent of his abilities. And there is plenty of evidence for this conclusion in the story.

Before resolving the inconsistencies, it's worth making clear exactly why Jon's two claims, the power of timeless foresight and the theory of fatalism, can't both be true, given certain events in the story. Take the three examples mentioned earlier about Jon's ability to learn new information and even be surprised by it. Normal people form beliefs based on the information that is available to them, and they change their beliefs when they gain new information. But if Jon has timeless perception, it is impossible for him to know anything at time A that he did not know at time B. This means that his beliefs at times A and B should be identical. This should also mean, of course, that it is impossible to surprise him. When Laurie confronts him on exactly this point, mentioning that he was surprised when told that his acquaintances were getting cancer, he answers by saying, "Everything is preordained. Even my responses."[10] Yet this is a completely nonsensical response to her question. He is saying that for some reason, he responded with surprise without *being* surprised. Free will or no free will, it's completely mysterious why such a response would be elicited without a change in knowledge.

The other major inconsistency in the story is Jon's inability to foresee Adrian Veidt's plan. Of course, the story *supposedly* has an explanation: Adrian's tachyon generators produced some disturbance that inhibited Jon's ability to see the future. Unfortunately, this explanation is total hogwash. If the tachyon generators work as described, they could have obscured some period of time from Jon's gaze—let's say, two years (Adrian presumably prepared this plan well in advance of its climax). Let's also suppose that the tachyons successfully prevent Jon from detecting Adrian's plan during this time. Yet if Jon's perception of time is like a nonbranching movie (since he believes in fatalism), he would have *always known* that this two-year period of obscurity existed. Since he claims to see the past, the present, and the future all at once, anything he knows after the cloudy period ends would be known to him before the cloudy period began. Since he learns the details of Adrian's plan by the end of the story, he would have had this knowledge prior to the cloudy period.

Tripping on Tachyons

Just when things were looking bad for Alan Moore's credibility as a sci-fi writer, a solution presents itself. The tachyons clouded Jon's knowledge of the future, but they seem to have affected him in other ways as well. He shows signs of disorientation several times during the story, notably toward the end. For instance, when addressing Laurie in Antarctica, he accidentally starts speaking to Rorschach ninety seconds in the future, subsequently admitting that the tachyons are "muddling things up."[11] Dan even comments that Jon seems "drugged or something," which might be exactly right.

Perhaps the best interpretation of chapter IV, when Jon is having his peculiar flashbacks, is not that this is how he always experiences time, but rather that the tachyons are causing some sort of weird "acid trip." This would explain why Laurie is surprised by Jon's behavior so many times throughout the story. I mean, really, she's been living with this guy for years, right? Why would she be surprised by his shtick if he *typically* acts like this? His habit of informing Laurie of her future actions, his claiming that he's on Mars when he isn't,[12] his—*hurm*—"enhanced" love-making[13]: these are all behavioral oddities that Laurie has never seen before. The way to reconcile Jon's inconsistencies in the story is to assume that the disorienting tachyons are causing him to lose his bearings and have an exaggerated opinion of his own abilities. The fact that he can be surprised and can change his mind (as he does regarding the value of human life in chapter IX) illustrates that he does not have infallible foresight.

It's possible that fatalism is indeed true, and that he's just got very limited foresight. It's also possible that he has quite extensive foresight, but that fatalism is false. Perhaps he's always seen time as a nonbranching movie reel, although it in fact branches. All we know is that since Jon's foresight definitely has limitations, we don't need to accept fatalism.

Do as I Say, Not as I Blue

So if you run into Dr. Manhattan, you should have plenty of worries, but the loss of your free will isn't one of them. Though it seems as if *Watchmen* is setting up the inconsistency of free will and foreknowledge, there are neat little clues in the story that get us out of trouble. Theological fatalism is another matter, however—when it comes to *God's* foreknowledge, the debate rages on. Does God exist outside of time? If so, how would God interact with entities like us who are inside of time? If God's knowledge is timeless, is he looking at a branching or a nonbranching movie reel? Thank goodness, all *we* have to worry about is the big, blue, naked guy!

NOTES

1. *Watchmen*, chap. IX, p. 5.

2. See Boethius, *The Consolation of Philosophy*, written in 524 (New York: Macmillan, 1962), Book V, Prose vi; and Aquinas, *Summa Theologica*, written between 1265 and 1274 (New York: Benzinger Brothers, 1947), Article 13.

3. For an extended discussion of this problem, see Linda Zagzebski's entry on "Foreknowledge and Free Will," in *The Stanford Encyclopedia of Philosophy*, http://plato.stanford.edu/archives/spr2008/entries/free-will-foreknowledge.

4. *Watchmen*, chap. IV, p. 11.

5. William Paley, *Natural Theology*, with an introduction and notes by Matthew D. Eddy and David M. Knight (1802; repr., Oxford: Oxford University Press, 2006).

6. *Watchmen*, chap. XII, p. 27.

7. Ibid., chapter IX, p. 6. See also chapter 9 in this book, "A Timely Encounter: Dr. Manhattan and Henri Bergson" by Christopher M. Drohan, for more on Dr. Manhattan's perception of time.

8. Ibid., chap. IV, p. 16.

9. Ibid., chap. IX, p. 5.

10. Ibid.

11. Ibid., chap. XII, p. 11.

12. Ibid., chap. VII, p. 23.

13. Ibid., chap. III, p. 4.

I'M JUST A PUPPET WHO CAN SEE THE STRINGS: DR. MANHATTAN AS A STOIC SAGE

Andrew Terjesen

It's hard to imagine how Dr. Manhattan sees the world. We are tempted to think he has lost his humanity and has moved beyond our simple philosophies. The way that Dr. Manhattan talks about the world, however, sounds very much like the philosophical school of *Stoicism*. Indeed, his development through the course of *Watchmen* illustrates the development of a twenty-first-century Stoic sage.

The Modern Misunderstanding of Stoicism

When people hear the word *stoic* today, they tend to think of a person who shows "indifference to pleasure and pain; repressing all feeling."[1] And that seems to fit Dr. Manhattan to a *t*. Throughout *Watchmen*, he seems indifferent to the emotions and needs of those around him, even the people he claims to care about. Just think of when he whisks Laurie to Mars for a conversation, and she begins to suffocate because of the lack of atmosphere. Finally, after she stumbles around a bit, he rectifies the problem, saying, "Please forgive me. . . . Sometimes these things slip my mind."[2] Janey Slater, his ex-girlfriend, sums up his problem, saying, he "know[s] how every damn thing in this world fits together except people! He couldn't relate to me. Not emotionally."[3]

Stoicism became associated with emotional indifference because that is one of the things that Stoics recommend. The goal for Stoics was to achieve a state of *apatheia* (this term is related to the English word *apathy*, although there is a major difference, as we'll see shortly), which literally means to be "without passions."[4] In associating *stoic* with *dispassionate*, we have done a disservice to Stoicism, because we omit the reason *why* they advocate a state of apatheia. Consider the words of Seneca (4 BCE–65 CE) when he said, "Our first need is not to become angry, our second to stop being angry, our third to cure anger in others."[5] This is not controversial—we often encourage people to get rid of (or at least manage) their anger. Certainly, the goal of Rorschach's therapist was to help Rorschach get beyond his anger and other violent emotions.[6]

But why is anger such a negative emotion? Because of what we do when we're angry. Consider the Comedian. When the Vietnamese woman he impregnated gets angry at the fact that he is abandoning her and she cuts him, her action enrages him to the point where he shoots her.[7] Both of them acted in anger and did things that we would deem wrong (although obviously his actions were much worse than hers).

But anger is not the only emotion that leads us to do harmful things. Janey's love for Jon leads her to treat Laurie very poorly when she first meets her. And Ozymandias cares so much about humanity that he is willing to sacrifice a large number of people for the sake of everyone else. Negative emotions are not the only emotions that lead to bad or immoral results.

The Stoic view is that *all* emotions are irrational judgments about the world. Chrysippus (circa 280–207 BCE) is reported to have said, "We say that such people are irrationally moved, not as though they make a bad calculation, which would be the sense opposite to 'reasonably,' but rather in the sense of a rejection of reason."[8] The rejection of reason that Chrysippus describes is not meant in the sense of someone who is out of control, but rather someone who chooses to believe something other than what reason says is true. Stoics define anger as "a desire for revenge on one who seems to have done an injustice inappropriately."[9]

In the modern era, we tend to focus on the "desire for revenge" part of anger and neglect the fact that anger comes with a belief that we have been treated inappropriately. When the Comedian shoots the Vietnamese woman, he acts as if she had no right to cut him the way she did. All emotions are accompanied by beliefs about the world that make them the emotions that they are. Janey's love for Dr. Manhattan is accompanied by a belief that he is the only person she should be involved with (and vice versa). Stoics argue that these beliefs are false. So our emotions reject reason in the sense that they refuse to accept the truth about the world. Given how the Comedian treated his lover, her actions are not completely unjustified; nor is it the case that Dr. Manhattan is the only person that Janey could ever be with.

The Stoic's point is that negative emotions lead us to do bad things because they are based on a misunderstanding of the world. But negative emotions aren't the only emotions that do this. Positive emotions such as love also give a distorted view of the world. Now, one might not object to positive self-delusion; after all, there seems to be no harm in thinking that things are better than they are. But the potential for disaster does indeed lurk in the loss of those things that we think are better than they are. Janey's fear of losing Dr. Manhattan turns her love into jealousy, and the actual loss of Dr. Manhattan leads her to a bitterness that sets the stage for her later betrayal of him. Emotions are not bad because they cloud our judgment; they are bad because they involve a misleading perception of the world. So, we should seek to cure ourselves of the delusions of emotion, just as Rorschach should free himself from paranoid delusions.

"I Read Atoms": Seeing Nature for What It Is

If we are going to label our emotions "delusional," we need to have a sense of what reality is. For the Stoics, there is only one obvious candidate for reality—the natural world. Therefore, a Stoic needs to focus on what is found in nature, as opposed to what is put there by human beings. As an example of this Stoic perspective, consider Dr. Manhattan's reaction to the death of the Comedian. He says simply and stoically, "A live body and a dead body contain the same number of particles. Structurally, there is no discernible difference."[10] This statement may be unfeeling, but it's also true.

Our emotions often lead us to believe that a particular person is special and should not die like everyone else. Epictetus (c. 55–135) offers various bits of advice in order to help people see nature for what it is. One of his gems is:

> Never say of anything, "I have lost it"; but, "I have returned it." Is your child dead? It is returned. Is your wife dead? She is returned. Is your estate taken away? Well, and is not that likewise returned? "But he who took it away is a bad man." What difference is it to you who the giver assigns to take it back? While he gives it to you to possess, take care of it; but don't view it as your own, just as travelers view a hotel.[11]

This may seem pretty harsh, but Epictetus's point is that everything in the world lives and dies, and there is nothing we can do to change that. By coming to terms with the fact that we cannot control who lives and who dies or when they die, we can avoid unnecessary anguish. And instead of worrying about when our loved ones will die, we will take pleasure in them while we can and savor every moment with them.

That last part may seem a bit contradictory, since the Stoics have made it clear that all positive emotions are irrational judgments. There is a difference, however, between taking joy in a child because it is your child and taking the perspective of nature and recognizing that it is "good" to see the species continue. We see Dr. Manhattan react this way when Janey gives him a ring. He says, "I like it very much. Its atomic structure is a perfect grid, like a checkerboard."[12] This response bothers Janey because it seems so unemotional. But Dr. Manhattan is appreciating the object as an object—and the pleasant symmetry in nature—and not appreciating it through the lens of sentimentality. Even from an unsentimental perspective, things can be appreciated.

From what we have seen, it should not be surprising that for Stoics, "the goal of life is to live in agreement with nature, which is to live according to virtue. For nature leads to virtue."[13] Stoics go so far as to claim that the only truly good thing is virtue and the only truly bad thing is vice. Everything else in the universe is simply "indifferent"—neither good nor bad. So, for the Stoics, seeing the death of the Comedian as part of a natural cycle is good, refusing to see his death as inevitable is bad, and the death itself is neither good nor bad.

This aspect of Stoicism is very difficult to accept, but it makes more sense if you consider what it means to say that virtue is good and vice is bad. The good is something that we should strive after no matter what, and likewise, the bad is something we should avoid no matter what. So, as the Stoics see it, we should be willing to sacrifice ourselves in the pursuit of virtue and we should be upset at vice. Dr. Manhattan's initial reaction to Laurie's affair is not very stoical, but it also reveals why the Stoics consider human relationships neither bad nor good, but indifferent. When Laurie first asks Dr. Manhattan to save the world, he refuses, saying, "You were my only link. My only concern with the world."[14] Dr. Manhattan is willing to allow an entire planet to be sacrificed because he has been betrayed by one particular person. But no human being is worth sacrificing the world; what should matter is whether the world should continue to exist, not whether some particular part of it is worth saving or destroying.

Of course, from the perspective of nature, not everything is equal. To a human being, oxygen is necessary for survival, while carbon monoxide is toxic. Thus, oxygen is valuable inasmuch as it keeps humans alive, and as long as humans are a part of nature, oxygen will be a valuable thing for humans. Stoics would refer to oxygen in the case of humans (and other beings) as a *preferred* thing and carbon monoxide as *dispreferred*.[15] Virtue, for the Stoics, is knowing the way of nature and consequently knowing what is to be preferred and dispreferred in particular cases. Children are to be preferred if a species is to continue, and practical concerns lead to parents preferring the survival of their own children.

Dr. Manhattan Does Get Upset, So He's Not Really a Stoic, Right?

Based on the description so far, it does not seem that Dr. Manhattan acts very stoically. Aside from his petulant refusal to help Earth, there are a number of other times where he seems to act emotionally. When he first hears that several of his former associates, including Janey Slater, have developed cancer, he seems very upset.[16] And when he finally "learns" that Laurie slept with Dan Dreiberg, he is angry and hurt.[17] On the face of it, these seem like very unstoical reactions.

That is true, however, only if we stick with a very broad interpretation of *emotion*.

The Stoic understanding of emotion is narrower than our
sense of the word might suggest. Seneca, for example, argued
that an emotion happens only when we are consciously caught
up in a feeling that misrepresents the way the world is. By
defining emotion this way, Seneca excluded some states that
we often identify with emotion. For example, we previously
referred to the Vietnamese woman who attacked the Comedian
as having acted in anger, but that is not entirely correct. The
Comedian was complicit in an act that left her socially vulner-
able, and he made it clear he wanted nothing to do with her.
In nature, it is preferred that parents tend to their offspring
(as well as form a connection with their partners), and the
Comedian refuses to do that. He acts in a manner that goes
against nature and is therefore irrational.

To feel a desire to punish someone who has *actually* done
you wrong would not be anger. Anger is when we refuse to be
reasonable in our actions. As Seneca said, "If [the feeling] lis-
tens to reason and follows where it is led, it is no longer anger,
the hallmark of which is willful disobedience . . . if it accepts
a limit, it needs some other name, having ceased to be anger,
which I understand to be something unbridled and ungov-
erned."[18] When the Vietnamese woman attacks the Comedian,
she makes it clear that this is a form of punishment for his
dismissing her; she did not plan to do anything more than give
him a reminder of what he had done wrong. This is in contrast
to the Comedian's entirely excessive response, which fails to
recognize that she had a legitimate grievance with him.

Similarly, Dr. Manhattan's concern for those whom he
might have given cancer is not really the kind of emotion that
the Stoics condemn. He may have been responsible for their
cancer, and it is important for him to act on this information to
see whether he poses a continued threat. In addition, to be "sad-
dened" at (or to disprefer) the loss of someone due to cancer

is not entirely irrational, as that person's companionship was preferred because we are naturally social creatures. The point at which Dr. Manhattan's feelings become unacceptable is when they segue into excessive impulses that cause him to act against the natural order (for example, if he had tried to resurrect people from the dead, rather than looking for a new companion among the billions of still-living humans).

But this still does not account for Dr. Manhattan's outburst at Laurie, which does reveal an irrational anger. Not only is Laurie an adult who can make choices for herself, but she was also growing dissatisfied with the relationship. Seneca describes the onset of anger in the following way: "The first movement is involuntary, a preparation as it were, for emotion, a kind of threat. The next is voluntary but not insistent—I may, for example, think it right for me to wreak vengeance because I have been harmed. . . . The third is really out of control; wanting retribution not just 'if it is right' but at all costs."[19] Our initial responses to things are out of control. Dr. Manhattan cannot help but be angry when he discovers Laurie's affair. After that initial response, there is the moment when he thinks, She betrayed me. But once he's had that thought, the Stoics say he must submit it to reason and try to determine whether it is a justified response. Dr. Manhattan, upon reflection, realizes all of the ways in which he has failed Laurie, and so he does not retaliate against her for the affair. He acts like a good Stoic; once the initial impulse has passed, his reason comes in and prevents him from acting inappropriately.[20]

So, Stoics don't dismiss everything we think of as emotion. Rather, Stoics dismiss a very specific kind of emotion, the state of consciously surrendering oneself to an inaccurate representation of one's situation.[21] Seneca said, "Emotion is not a matter of being moved by impressions received, but of surrendering oneself to them and following up the chance movements."[22] By Seneca's definition, Dr. Manhattan's initial feeling of betrayal is not an emotion; it is an impulse. But if he had chosen to keep feeling that Laurie had betrayed him, then he would be experiencing what Stoics mean by an "emotion." Stoicism is a lot more accepting of human weakness than most people realize; after all, that is a part of human nature and therefore the cycle of nature.

Stoicism and Fate: A Puppet Comes to Terms with the Strings

Dr. Manhattan's Stoic attitude derives from the fact that he can see the workings of the world in a way that we cannot. He can see the complex interrelationships of particles in the universe. When he first reforms himself, he states, "It's just a question of reassembling the components into the correct sequence."[23] The ability to see all of the patterns of nature would make it much easier for one to conclude that nature has an intricate design that we should follow. And certainly, if one looks at atomic structures, rather than at surface appearances, one is more likely to see things as they are: endless rearrangements of particles over time.

Dr. Manhattan's Stoicism is also aided by his experience of time. For him, everything is happening at once. The past, the present, and the future all dissolve into one moment. As a result, he is constantly aware of the long-term patterns of our actions and also knows how things will work out. Unlike the rest of us, he knows that he cannot change the future. As he says, "I can't prevent the future. To me, it's already happening."[24] That feeling would drive some people mad, but Dr. Manhattan accepts it stoically. Rather than trying to fight fate, he accepts that everything is preordained, including how he responds. As he notes, "I'm just a puppet who can see the strings."[25] Dr. Manhattan thus embraces his place in the cosmic order and continues with his life.[26]

Fate, though, is a thorny issue for Stoics. On the one hand, Stoics believe that nature follows rules that create certain patterns of existence. On the other hand, they hold that people "choose" whether to accept the way the world is. If these choices, as Dr. Manhattan says, are also preordained, then it seems strange to say that someone is praiseworthy for choosing to accept the way things are. And according to Dr. Manhattan, our responses are not under our control: they were determined long ago. His view is shared by some Stoics but not all. The question of free will versus determinism is a vexing issue in philosophy, and the Stoics had no more success in settling it than anyone else has.

The Stoics had a reason, though, for not worrying too much about the question of determinism, and it explains why they could embrace being puppets on a string: the belief that "the cosmos is administered by mind and providence."[27] In fact, the Stoic God is described as "an animal, immortal, rational, perfect in happiness, immune to everything bad, providentially [looking after] the cosmos and things in the cosmos."[28] This view is very helpful in justifying the Stoic ethical perspective. The idea is that we should act in accordance with nature because that is the same as acting in accordance with the will of a perfectly rational being. And we should accept everything that happens because no matter how awful it might seem, it is part of some divine plan for the universe as a whole (a view echoed in many religious traditions today). In the story of *Watchmen*, Ozymandias tries to assume this role because he thinks that only he is smart enough to save the world. But Ozymandias is still very human, and it's not clear by the end that his actions were the best thing for the universe as a whole.

Thermodynamic Miracles and the "Good Emotions"

Although Dr. Manhattan is stoical throughout *Watchmen*, he does not achieve sagehood until his conversation on Mars. The Stoic *sage* is the model that all Stoics try to emulate, as it represents someone who truly understands the nature of the universe. With that perfect understanding, the sage has developed a new set of emotions that the Stoics call *eupatheia* (literally, "good passions"). These good passions are the only feelings that a true Stoic should have, and it is not possible for them to be felt by anyone except a sage, who appreciates what is truly valuable in the world.

At the beginning of Dr. Manhattan's conversation with Laurie on Mars, he exhibits Stoic indifference—not just in forgetting that she needs air, but also in statements such as "human life is brief and mundane."[29] Though we might not like to think of it that way, in the cosmic scheme of things, he is right. His Stoic indifference makes it difficult for him to see any reason to become involved in stopping a nuclear Armageddon. After all, if the human race were annihilated, the universe would continue and some other species would take the place of human beings. In fact, the only reason that Dr. Manhattan gives for acting is a very unstoical one: that he cares for Laurie in particular. And tellingly, the loss of this personal connection makes it possible for him to become a Stoic sage.

Rather than basing the value of humanity on the value he places on one particular person, he shifts to seeing the value of all humanity as a result of its place in the universe. Laurie tries to convince him to act by appealing to the inherent value of life (and human creative achievement), but he dismisses it as a "highly overrated phenomenon" and replies that the universe could carry on just fine without life.[30] Laurie's approach had been to focus on the aftereffects of the universe, whereas Dr. Manhattan is impressed by the system itself. Look at his final moment of revelation:

Dr. Manhattan: Thermodynamic miracles . . . events with odds against so astronomical they're effectively impossible, like oxygen spontaneously becoming gold. I long to observe such a thing. And yet, in each human coupling, a thousand million sperm vie for a single egg. Multiply those odds by countless generations, against the odds of your ancestors being alive; meeting; siring this precise son; that exact daughter until your mother loves a man she has every reason to hate, and of that union, of the thousand million children competing for fertilization, it was you, only you, that emerged. To distill so specific a form from that chaos of improbability . . . the thermodynamic miracle.

Laurie: But if me, my birth, if that's a thermodynamic miracle . . . I mean, you could say that about anybody in the world!

Dr. Manhattan: Yes. Anybody in the world. But the world is so full of people, so crowded with these miracles, that they become commonplace and we forget. . . . I forget.[31]

Dr. Manhattan's realization that the existence of the human race is (in Stoic terms) to be "preferred" occurs when he reflects on the system that brought each person into existence, and he marvels at what it does. The pleasure he takes in the fact that the universe is constructed to bring about so many thermodynamic miracles is a kind of pleasure reserved only for the Stoic sage. The Stoics called this *joy*, and it is one of three "good emotions" that the sage possesses, the other two being *caution* and *wish*.[32] They are good impulses because they are grounded in reason, and, since the sage has a perfect understanding of the universe, they do not misrepresent the universe in any way. Dr. Manhattan's Stoic joy at the thermodynamic miracle is replaced by a Stoic wish to preserve that miracle as much as possible.

Stoicism without a Rational Lawgiver?

But there is one significant way in which Dr. Manhattan's realization is a departure from ancient Stoicism. When

Dr. Manhattan takes Stoic joy in the thermodynamic miracle, he does not view it as the work of a perfectly rational creator. At one point he thinks, "Perhaps nothing is made. Perhaps it simply is, has been, will always be there. A clock without a craftsman."[33] What really astounds him about those thermodynamic miracles is how they seem to come about by chance.

The idea of a rational creator is intimately bound up with ancient Stoicism. But Stoicism had a revival after the Renaissance, during which it changed enough in response to the "modern" world that it is referred to as Neo-Stoicism. René Descartes (1596–1650), regarded as the father of modern philosophy, had Neo-Stoic leanings. In a letter to Princess Elisabeth of Bohemia (1596–1662), Descartes told her that the only way to cope with her misfortunes was to live a life founded upon reason, because "the true function of reason, then, in the conduct of life is to examine and consider without passion the value of all the perfections, both of the body and of the soul, which can be acquired by our conduct."[34] Descartes also believed that the foundation of his Neo-Stoicism was the belief in an omnipotent and omnibenevolent creator—so, in that respect, it was not a major departure from the ancient Stoics.

Descartes' Neo-Stoicism influenced a number of thinkers, however, including Baruch Spinoza (1632–1677), who believed that the only thing that existed was God (which he equated with Nature, similar to the ancient Stoics) and that everything else was a part of God. Since Nature was God, then it only made sense that our natural impulses were divinely inspired. As Spinoza said, "To act in absolute conformity with virtue is nothing else in us but to act, to live, to preserve one's own being (these three things mean the same) under the guidance of reason on the basis of seeking one's own advantage."[35] This is a very Stoic thing to say. But in contrast to Descartes and the ancient Stoics, Spinoza had a conception of God (informed as it was by developing science) that was not a personal one. Instead, "God" was the laws of Nature that kept everything going.

It may seem like a small difference, but all of the Stoics prior to Spinoza (including Descartes) equated the divine administrator with a Zeus-like figure who watched over us and made sure everything worked out for the best. Spinoza's God was completely impersonal and indifferent to the universe. But even though Spinoza's God does not care about any particular part of the universe, Spinoza's notion of God embodies all of the laws that the universe must follow in order to exist. And since God is perfect, the laws of the universe must be perfectly rational as well. And if those laws are perfectly rational, then a life based on them will be rational, too. Spinoza has given us natural laws without requiring that there be a Lawgiver to set everything in motion.

At the end of *Watchmen*, Dr. Manhattan tells Ozymandias that he plans to leave this galaxy and perhaps create some thermodynamic miracles of his own. Assuming that Dr. Manhattan has reached a complete understanding of nature, he might be assuming the role of the ancient Stoic God (not something the Stoics could have envisioned, but then again neither is Dr. Manhattan!). He was only able to do so, however, because some thermodynamic miracle led to the creation of Dr. Manhattan. The idea that the universe is constructed of inherently rational laws would actually help to answer the question that always confronts the old Stoic God: where did he come from and how did he know what the rational thing to do was? It seems that a rational universe needs to precede a rational being. Dr. Manhattan's Stoicism could take things a step further from the Neo-Stoicism of Descartes and Spinoza. Even Spinoza seemed to take it for granted that a rational Universe had to exist, without explaining how it came about. Appealing to more modern ideas such as quantum mechanics and evolution, Dr. Manhattan might conclude that the very first thermodynamic miracle was the beginning of structure and order in the universe—that it was not preordained or guaranteed to continue—and that ever since, the universe has been tweaking the rules it lives by in order to create a self-sustaining universe of immense complexity.

"Relax and See the Whole Continuum"

Regardless of how the universe came to be the way it is, the Stoics' point—the one that Dr. Manhattan came to see on the surface of Mars—is that the universe is too well-structured to be ignored, and the fact that it has kept things going for billions of years suggests that we should pay more attention to its workings as we organize our lives. And we should definitely not let our feelings overtake us and cause us to lose sight of how well things can work out. Even when they don't seem to work out, as when Nite Owl and the others fail to stop Ozymandias from saving the world, the universe seems to correct for it. And the fact that the universe is governed by these laws does not make it any less miraculous. As Dr. Manhattan observes, "We gaze continually at the world and it grows dull in our perceptions. Yet seen from another's vantage point, as if new, it may still take the breath away."[36] Stoicism is about stepping out of our particular perspective and seeing the bigger picture. Once we've relaxed and abandoned our petty emotional hang-ups, we can really appreciate the relatively harmonious operations of the universe as a whole. After the Stoic sage Dr. Manhattan's epiphany about thermodynamic miracles, it's what he can see and take joy in. Shouldn't we all?

NOTES

1. *Oxford English Dictionary, Second Edition.*

2. *Watchmen*, chap. IX, p. 3.

3. Ibid., chap. III, pp. 5–6.

4. "They say the wise man is also free of passions," in Diogenes Laertius, *Lives of the Philosophers*, Book VII, chap. 117. Unless otherwise noted, all quotes from Stoic philosophers (other than Seneca) can be found in Brad Inwood and L. P. Gerson, *Hellenistic Philosophy: Introductory Readings, 2nd ed.* (Indianapolis: Hackett Publishing, 1997).

5. Seneca, "On Anger," in *Moral and Political Essays*, ed. John M. Cooper and J. F. Procope (Cambridge, UK: Cambridge University Press, 1995), Book III, chap. 5, section 2.

6. Dr. Malcolm Long describes Rorschach as a "classic case of misdirected aggression" (*Watchmen*, chap. VI, p. 11).

7. *Watchmen*, chap. II, pp. 14–15. Although, from a Stoic point of view, the Vietnamese woman's reaction might not be considered anger—as we'll see in a later section.

8. As quoted by Galen, *On the Doctrines of Hippocrates and Plato*, IV, 18, in Inwood and Gerson, *Hellentic Philosophy*.

9. Diogenes Laertius, *Lives of the Philosophers*, Book VII, chap. 113.

10. *Watchmen*, chap. I, p. 21.

11. Epictetus, *Enchiridion*, chap. 11, trans. Elizabeth Carter, http://classics.mit.edu/Epictetus/epicench.html.

12. *Watchmen*, chap. IV, p. 11.

13. Diogenes Laertius, *Lives of the Philosophers*, Book VII, chap. 87.

14. *Watchmen*, chapter IX, p. 8.

15. Diogenes Laertius, *Lives of the Philosophers*, Book VII, chap. 105.

16. *Watchmen*, chap. III, p. 14.

17. Ibid., chap. IX, p. 8.

18. Seneca, Book I, chap. 9, sections 2–3.

19. Seneca, Book II, chap. 4, section 1.

20. Stoics call this initial impression *prosphaton*—a word that was used to describe the smell of fish in the market before it has spoiled. The idea is that the *prosphaton* is something you can't avoid and it initially hits you very strongly, but it is not yet something that has gone bad. After all, prepare the fish properly and it will smell and taste great; but if you just leave it there, do nothing with it, and let it rot, it will turn into something awful.

21. Any other time Dr. Manhattan mentions the affair (even when it is chronologically earlier than Laurie's "revelation"), he does not seem upset, presumably because once he is out of the moment, he has come to see the part he played in this (and maybe remembers what he did to Janey).

22. Seneca, Book II, chap. 3, section 1.

23. *Watchmen*, chap. IV, p. 9.

24. Ibid., p. 16.

25. Ibid., chap. IX, p. 5.

26. For more on the topic of Dr. Manhattan's perception of time, see chapter 9 of this book, "A Timely Encounter: Dr. Manhattan and Henri Bergson," by Christopher M. Drohan.

27. Diogenes Laertius, *Lives of the Philosophers*, Book VII, chap. 138.

28. Ibid., chap. 147.

29. *Watchmen*, chap. IX, p. 17.

30. Ibid., p. 13.

31. Ibid., pp. 26–27.

32. Joy is taking pleasure in the only thing of value (which is virtue); caution is worrying about losing the only thing of value; and wish is desiring the only thing of value.

33. *Watchmen*, chap. IV, p. 28.

34. Descartes to Princess Elisabeth of Bohemia, September 1, 1645. Found in John Cottingham, et al., eds., *The Philosophical Writings of Descartes, Volume III: The Correspondence* (Cambridge, UK: Cambridge University Press, 1991), p. 265.

35. Quoted in Matthew Stewart, *The Courtier and the Heretic: Leibniz, Spinoza, and the Fate of God in the Modern World* (New York: W. W. Norton, 2006), pp. 101–102.

36. *Watchmen*, chap. IX, p. 27.

PART FOUR

THIS IS NOT YOUR FATHER'S COMIC BOOK

"WHY DON'T YOU GO READ A BOOK OR SOMETHING?" *WATCHMEN* AS LITERATURE

Aaron Meskin

Is *Watchmen* Literature?

In 2005, two critics at *Time* magazine picked *Watchmen* as one of the one hundred best English-language novels published since the magazine's founding.[1] But was this justified? Should a mere comic book—even one that is now sold in the graphic novel format—really be considered a great novel? Perhaps graphic novels are not really novels at all. After all, rubber ducks are not ducks, and Fakin' Bacon is not bacon.[2] Words can mislead. So we should not assume that graphic novels are novels just because of their name.

At the root of these concerns is the question of whether comics and graphic novels can count as literature. By common consensus, comics just don't get much better or more artistic than *Watchmen*. If there is a comics canon—a list of the great works in the art form that serves as a standard against which all other comics are judged—then surely *Watchmen* is at the core of that canon (along with such works as *Maus*, *The Dark Knight Returns*, *The Sandman*, and *Persepolis*).[3] It's certainly *complex* enough to count as literature—you could spend weeks figuring out all of the allusions in it.[4]

Moreover, it seems as if it *matters* whether graphic novels are literature. Comics and graphic novels don't get no respect. Well, maybe they get a little respect these days. Still, they don't get as much as they deserve. If some comics are literature, then it's possible that they and their readers might start getting their props. In addition, it seems that it would make a difference to our *appreciation* of graphic novels such as *Watchmen* if they were (and were recognized as) literature. For if they are literature, then it is probably a mistake to consider them to have *solely* entertainment value—literature is the sort of thing that invites us to look for both distinctive uses of language (metaphor, imagery, ambiguity, allusion) and significant content. That is, we read literature with an eye out for "literary" language and "deep" meanings. If *Watchmen* is literature, then it makes sense to read it that way, too.

Whom Do We Ask?

On the face of it, graphic novels such as *Watchmen* seem as if they probably *are* works of literature. They are often bought and sold in the same places as works of literature; they are bound like works of literature; they are full of words; we hold them in our hands and read them as we do works of literature; they are reviewed (at least nowadays) in many of the same magazines and newspapers that review literature; some of them are taught in literature classes; professors in literature departments write articles about them; and so on. The similarities between graphic novels and standard works of literature are striking.

But as philosophers never cease to remind us, even if something looks and quacks like a duck, it may not be a duck (it *could* be a shape-shifting supervillain in the guise of a duck or, more likely, a very sophisticated duck decoy). Similarity does not amount to identity. There's that old appearance versus reality distinction to worry about.[5] So the fact that graphic novels are *a lot like* works of literature does not guarantee that they *are* works of literature. And the fact that it would be a good thing if graphic novels counted as literature doesn't favor that view either—just because we (fans of comics) want something to be true doesn't make it so.

Nor can we settle the issue by turning to a dictionary. The *Oxford English Dictionary* offers a range of definitions of the term *literature*, but, alas, these do not settle the question of whether graphic novels in general (and *Watchmen* in particular) count as literature. In the first place, the OED offers five definitions of the term, so we will still be stuck trying to figure out which of the five definitions to use.[6] But more important, dictionaries just aren't the right types of authorities to settle such a question. Dictionaries tell us how people use words—they don't tell us what things *are*. And it looks like we need to figure out what literature *is*, not merely how people use the word *literature*.

We cannot decide the issue by turning to the experts. For one thing, it is not obvious which experts to turn to—do we want experts on comics, experts on literature, or both? But there is an even more pressing problem: insofar as we can find any experts on the matter, they would most likely disagree. The great comics artist Will Eisner (who originally popularized the term *graphic novel*) declared that "in every sense, this misnamed form of reading is entitled to be regarded as literature because the images are employed as a language."[7] On the other hand, Alan Moore himself (the author of *Watchmen*) has expressed skepticism about viewing comics in literary terms:

> With the best will in the world, if you try to describe the *Dazzler* graphic novel in the same terms as you describe

Moby Dick then you're simply asking for trouble. As opposed to films without movement or sound we get novels without scope, depth or purpose. That isn't good enough either. . . . Rather than seizing upon the superficial similarities between comics and films or comics and books in the hope that some of the respectability of those media will rub off upon us, wouldn't it be more constructive to focus our attention upon those ideas where comics are special and unique.[8]

But we can't rely on Alan Moore's say-so, since arguments by authorities are suspect (and, of course, *Watchmen* is a very different thing than the *Dazzler* graphic novel). Although Alan Moore *usually* knows the score, we can't assume that he always does. What to do, then? Unsurprisingly, I suggest that doing a little philosophy is the best way to settle the issue.

"Under the Hood" of Literature

Ever since Socrates (469–399 BCE), philosophers have been thinking and talking about "What is X?" issues: What is justice? What is truth? What is goodness? What is art? What is for lunch? (Okay, that last question isn't philosophical. But let me tell you, philosophers have been thinking and talking about it a lot over the last few millennia, and they still do today!) So the question "What is literature?" looks like just the sort of question that is ripe for philosophical investigation. In fact, this is exactly the type of question that philosophers of art (sometimes known as *aestheticians*) investigate.[9] And if we determine what literature is, then we should be able to figure out whether *Watchmen* and other graphic novels fall into that category.

In the broadest possible sense, the term *literature* is used to refer to pretty much any printed material. *Watchmen* clearly falls into this category, but so do campaign leaflets, newspaper inserts, and junk mail. Surely this is not the category that people are interested in when they debate the literary status of the graphic novel. The category is simply too wide to be of much interest or to shed light on our initial question about whether *Watchmen* deserves to stand among the one hundred greatest recent English-language novels.

The term *literature* is also sometimes used to refer to a body of written work that covers a specific topic. So, for example, there is the scientific literature on climate change, the literature on comic books (including this essay), and the literature on owls that Daniel Dreiberg (the second Nite Owl) refers to in his essay "Blood from the Shoulder of Pallas" (at the end of chapter VII of *Watchmen*). But this isn't the notion of literature that is of interest when we consider whether *Watchmen* is a work of literature, either. For one thing, this notion of literature seems to apply only (or at least mostly) to works of nonfiction. But *Watchmen*—thankfully—is a work of fiction.

Perhaps *Watchmen*'s fictionality is enough to make it literature. After all, many central cases of literature (the great novels and plays) are works of fiction. Of course, television shows and movies (including the long-awaited—or, for some of us, long-dreaded—*Watchmen* movie) are fiction, too, so mere fictionality is not enough to make something a work of literature. But what if we say that a work of literature is a written text that is also a fiction? That would exclude television shows and movies (although not screenplays), and it would seem to get things right. It includes the central works of literature—for example, novels by Dickens and Tolstoy and plays by Shakespeare and Ibsen—because they are written fictions, and it excludes written things that we know are not literature, such as technical manuals, history textbooks, and the essays in this very book, since these are not works of fiction.

The proposal to answer the "What is literature?" question that way will not work. You don't need to be as smart as Adrian Veidt to provide counterexamples to someone who tells you that literature is simply a fictional written text—some things are literature but are not written fictions, others are written fictions but are not literature. For one thing, the proposal is too broad; not every written fiction is a work of literature. There are fictions that are so basic and so bad that no one would be tempted to call them literature. When I wrote fictional stories for my seventh-grade English class, they did not count as literature. (Really—they were terrible.) No reasonable person would call them literature. And that's not because literature *must* be good. There's bad literature, after all. Nevertheless, being really bad must surely weigh against something's being literature. Similarly, most people would not count the romance novels published by Mills and Boon in the United Kingdom or by Harlequin Enterprises in North America as literature, even though they are fiction.[10] So being a written fiction is not, as they say in philosophy, a *sufficient condition* for being a work of literature, since simply being fictional does not *guarantee* that a written work is literature.

Nor is fictionality a *necessary condition* for literature, because it is not the case that something *must* be fictional in order to count as a work of literature. There are works that are widely recognized as literature that are not fictional—for example, various biographies and autobiographies such as *The Autobiography of Malcolm X*, *The Education of Henry Adams*, and *The Autobiography of Alice B. Toklas*. (Perhaps even Hollis Mason's autobiography, if we could see the whole thing!) So, again, literature cannot simply be a matter of fictional writing, because literature is not necessarily fictional.[11]

Opinions Are Like . . . Well, You Know!

At this point, the reader may be a bit skeptical of the task of finding some sort of objectively defensible account of what literature is. Maybe literary status is a matter of pure subjective opinion—one person's literature is another person's junk (and vice versa). Of taste and literature, the reader might think, one cannot really dispute. Maybe all there is to be said about whether *Watchmen* is literature is that it is if you think it is and it isn't if you think it isn't. But this won't do—such a subjectivist view about literature fails for a range of reasons. For one thing, it is clear that one *can* reasonably dispute whether something is literature. That is, people can and do argue and offer reasons for and against something's being literature. But if subjectivism were true, such arguments would make no sense. Furthermore, the subjectivist view implies that a person cannot be wrong about whether something is literature. But we are not infallible; we can make mistakes about whether something is literature. So the subjectivist view about literature looks implausible.

A related and somewhat more plausible view suggests that literary status is not, as the subjectivist would have it, a matter of what individuals think, but rather a matter of what a community or a culture thinks. Perhaps literary status is relative and something counts as literature, relative to a community or a culture, only when it is accepted as such by that community or culture. But I don't think this can be right, either. A community or a culture can certainly get things wrong—it can fail to recognize something that is literature as literature (as is arguably the case with comic books in our culture).

What to do? Do we have to sit down and try to perform the superheroic task of coming up with the right account of what literature is? Thankfully, I don't think we have to do that. Remember, our goal is to figure out whether *Watchmen* is literature. Getting the right account of literature would be a big help, but there are other ways we might determine whether the graphic novel counts as literature or not. Identification does not always require definition. Suppose we looked at a number of the most popular philosophical theories of what literature is and found that they all agreed that *Watchmen* did in fact count as literature. Well, then, I think we'd have a good

reason to consider it literature. And that, I suggest, is precisely
the situation we're in.

I'm not going to bore you with every theory of literature
that has ever been proposed by a philosopher or a literary
critic, but here are four important ones:

- The philosopher Monroe Beardsley (1915–1985) claimed that
  "literary discourse" is "discourse that is either an imitation
  illocutionary act or distinctly above the norm in its ratio of
  implicit to explicit meaning."[12]
- A bit more simply (albeit more problematically), the literary theorist Terry Eagleton thought all that could be
  said about literature was that it is "a highly valued kind of
  writing."[13]
- Peter Lamarque and Stein Haugom Olsen argued (roughly)
  that literary works are those works in which the author has
  intended to "invoke the literary response."[14]
- E. D. Hirsch famously suggested that he would define literature as "any text worthy to be taught to students by teachers
  of literature, when these texts are not being taught to students in other departments of a school or university."[15]

Some of these accounts are a bit unclear: an "imitation
illocutionary act" is Beardsley's way of talking about fiction,
and Lamarque and Olsen's "literary response" involves reading
a work in line with the standards of literature, that is, looking
for plot and theme and so on. Some of these accounts are not
entirely plausible: are all highly valued writings really literature, as Eagleton suggested? But that doesn't matter so much,
because it appears—at least on the face of it—that all of these
theories would count *Watchman* as literature. It's a fiction ("an
imitation illocutionary act"); it's a highly valued kind of writing; it's plausible that it was designed to invoke something like
a literary response; and it's certainly worthy of being taught in
literature classes. We don't have to decide which theory of literature is right, since all of them seem to agree that *Watchmen*

(and perhaps some other graphic novels) may count as literature. (*Dazzler*, you might have a shot!)

Some might think that treating comics as literature would be a bad thing because it would ignore their distinctive nature as comics. (This is one of the things Alan Moore warned us about in the passage previously quoted.) But we need not worry. Literature is a big tent and contains a number of art forms within it, such as poetry, the novel, and dramatic literature. Treating a poem as literature does not involve forgetting that it is a poem. Treating a novel as literature does not entail ignoring that it is a novel. Similarly, if *Watchmen* is literature, it is also a comic and should be recognized as such. But there's nothing odd or problematic about this.

There is one real problem, though. (Sorry, *Dazzler*.) All of the aforementioned accounts of literature appeal to the idea that works of literature are texts or discourse. But *Watchmen* is full of pictures! In fact, the pictures are incredibly important to it. It is a comic, after all. And leaving Dave Gibbons—who did the illustration and the lettering for the graphic novel—out of the picture (excuse the pun) seems like a big mistake. Maybe *Watchmen* isn't a literary work at all, since it isn't even a text or a discourse? But wait. . .

Do We Read *Watchmen* for the Pictures?

To dismiss *Watchmen* from the category of literature simply because it has pictures would be a mistake. A lot of literature has pictures. Think of the illustration in Dickens novels or the pictures in *Winnie the Pooh*. And there are forms of poetry, such as *concrete poetry*, in which the words of the poem itself make up some kind of picture. So merely having pictures is not enough to exclude something from the exalted category of the literary.

Note also that these examples show that treating a graphic novel like *Watchmen* as literature will not necessarily lead us to ignore its visual elements. Illustrated literature is literature, and treating it as such is not a mistake, nor does it involve forgetting that it is illustrated. If *Watchmen* is literature, then we should treat it as literature.

But *Watchmen* doesn't merely have a lot of pictures—the pictures are essential to it. In fact, some people might say that the pictures and the layout are ultimately the most important thing in a comic book, and in this comic book in particular. I would disagree with this, but I see where they're coming from, because in *Watchmen* the pictures are *really* important. Think of all of the purely visual elements of the book: the repeated image of the smiley face pins, the clock imagery, the visual symmetries in chapter V of the book, the extended sequences without—or almost without—words, such as the scene of Rorschach investigating the Comedian's death in chapter I, and so on. That's not what ordinary literature is like.

Layout is also crucial in *Watchmen*, whereas it is not typically important in standard works of literature. Your standard novel can be laid out in a variety of different ways—in 200 long pages or 400 short pages or 300 medium-size pages—without any significant artistic change. But if you changed the layout of *Watchmen* (e.g., printed the graphic novel in two-thirds or one-half the number of pages), you would likely lose significant artistic effects, such as the surprise created by the appearance of Rorschach on page 4 of chapter V. For example, imagine that page 3 and page 4 of that chapter were printed facing each other, rather than back-to-back—the effect of seeing Rorschach after the "BeHinD you" note would not be nearly as strong.

Another essential aspect of the book to consider is the lettering. As any devoted comic book reader will tell you, letterers count among the artists of standard comic books. In *Watchmen*, Dave Gibbons is credited as both illustrator and letterer. And so it makes sense to say that the lettering in *Watchmen* is, in fact, a part of the artwork itself. This is a major difference from standard works of literature, even works of illustrated literature. The people who select and set the typefaces for editions of ordinary novels are not considered to be among the artists who made those works. The typeface or the font in which a novel is published is simply not an artistic element of the novel itself. We can see this in the way that standard literary works allow for typesetting changes from edition to edition—the fonts in which they are printed are not essential to the work. But even when Adobe Illustrator is used in lettering (as is common now in mainstream comics), the specific way that a comic is lettered seems essential to it (and the person who uses the graphic software still counts among the artists who made the comic). Change the lettering in *Watchmen* (or replace it with a traditional mechanically produced font), and you have a different work, or so it would seem.

So, should we say that *Watchmen* is a work of literature, after all? I've pointed out some differences between comics and standard works of literature, but there is a lot to be said for continuing to treat *Watchmen* as a literary work. Aside from the general points I have made about graphic novels, there is the fact that *Watchmen* itself seems to allude to many works of literature and literary theory. "Fearful Symmetry" (the title of chapter V) almost certainly alludes to William Blake's poem "The Tyger" (which starts "Tyger Tyger, burning bright,/In the forests of the night;/ What immortal hand or eye,/Could frame thy fearful symmetry?"), and it may also allude to a book about Blake by the famous English literary critic Northrop Frye.[16]

In addition, the graphic novel makes at least two allusions to the famous author and heroin addict William S. Burroughs: *Nova Express*—a magazine that plays a significant role in the events that take place in *Watchmen*—is named after a book of that name by Burroughs, and Adrian Veidt (who appears to own the aforementioned magazine) mentions Burroughs at the beginning of chapter XI when talking about his television-viewing habits. In fact, Veidt's superhero name, Ozymandias, is the title of a famous poem by Percy Bysshe Shelley, and a line from that poem is used as the title of chapter XI and quoted at more length toward the end of the chapter. These allusions (along with Moore's oft-cited remark that he wanted to make "a super-hero *Moby Dick*") suggest that *Watchmen* is intended to be seen as connected in significant ways to important works of literature. The fancy "literary" language that Moore uses at times (such as in Dr. Manhattan's soliloquy in chapter IV) and the book's deep ethical and political themes also push us in that direction. So maybe it really is literature.

Watchmen as Hybrid

Comic books and graphic novels are hybrid art forms that come from the "interbreeding" between two or more different kinds of art forms, technologies, genres, or artistic media.[17] In this way, they are like other hybrid art forms such as opera, rock opera, and concrete poetry, all of which came about from combining various art forms or media. Comics were born in the nineteenth century by mixing the art forms of literature, print-making, caricature, and pictorial narrative. And "true graphic novels" such as *Watchmen* (as opposed to trade paperbacks that simply collect a short run or a single story arc out of an extended series) are a sort of double hybrid, coming from the interbreeding of the hybrid art form of comics with the literary genre of the novel.[18]

These claims about the hybrid nature, or *hybridity*, of comics and graphic novels are historical ones, and they are controversial.[19] But I think they are correct—they seem to offer a very natural explanation for why we seem to feel a pull in both directions about whether comics and graphic novels count as works of literature. Their hybridity, I suggest, explains the way that the question of *Watchmen*'s literary status seems so difficult to answer with confidence. It explains why comics and graphic novels are so much like literature and also why they are so much like nonliterary artworks, such as limited edition prints.

Suppose I'm right, and the art form of comics is a hybrid. That unfortunately does not settle the question of whether comics in general and *Watchmen* in particular are literature. Some—but not all—hybrids fall into *ancestral* categories. That is, some artistic hybrids still count as examples of the categories that they're descended from. Concrete poetry is still poetry and shaped canvasses still count as paintings. Other hybrids do not fall into ancestral categories—this is typically the case with biological hybrids (mules are not horses, and tangelos are not tangerines). So determining that comics and graphic novels descended from literature doesn't settle whether particular instances are literature. Furthermore, I suspect that Alan Moore is right about the *Dazzler* graphic novel. As much as I'm a fan of that disco superheroine (I still have some copies of *Dazzler* #1 in a plastic bag at my parents' house), I just don't think it counts as literature. But that doesn't settle the *Watchmen* question, either; it might be the case that some comics and graphic novels are literature and others are not.

So, Is *Watchmen* Literature or Not?

I think the right answer to the question of whether *Watchmen* is literature is that it is probably indeterminate. That is, there is no right or wrong answer to the question of whether the graphic novel fits into the category of literature. This would not be that surprising—borderline cases where it is indeterminate whether something falls into a category are all around us. So, for example, it might be indeterminate whether a man with a very small amount of hair on his head is bald, and it is plausibly indeterminate whether a woman who is 5'8" is tall. I think this is probably what's true about *Watchmen* and other graphic novels. The art form of comics is a hybrid one; graphic novels are plausibly double hybrids. Both art forms are descended from literature. Yet it just isn't determinately answerable whether they are literature or not.

But this doesn't matter. Remember the reasons it might matter whether *Watchmen* is literature—it is a matter of respect and of appreciation. If the graphic novel is literature, then it and its readers deserve respect. If it is literature, then it deserves to be read in a certain way. But we don't, in fact, need to establish that *Watchmen* is literature in order to reach these conclusions. If *Watchmen* is a valuable example of a hybrid art form—and it is!—then it deserves to be taken seriously. It doesn't need to be shown to be literature in order to establish its worth. And if graphic novels are descended from literature, then it is plausible that when they have literary elements (which *Watchmen* plausibly does), those elements deserve to be appreciated as literature.[20]

NOTES

1. Richard Lacayo and Lev Grossman, "All-Time 100 Novels," www.time.com/time/2005/100books/the_complete_list.html.

2. Fakin' Bacon is a surprisingly tasty vegetarian tempeh-based meat substitute.

3. For example, *Watchmen* is discussed extensively in Geoff Klock's *How to Read Superhero Comics and Why* (New York: Continuum, 2002) and Douglas Wolk's *Reading Comics: How Graphic Novels Work and What They Mean* (Cambridge, MA: Da Capo Press, 2007).

4. Or, if you're lazy like me, you could go online and check out one of the helpful sites where all of that research has been done for you (such as "The Annotated Watchmen" at www.capnwacky.com/rj/watchmen/.

5. Plato (429–347 BCE) addresses the appearance-reality distinction in his *Republic*, among other places. (See, for example, the allegory of the cave in Book VII of that dialogue or the discussion of the deceptive way an object looks in water in Book X.) And Western philosophy has been pretty much a series of footnotes to Plato. Or so it is said.

6. *The Oxford English Dictionary, Second Edition*, 1989, *OED Online* (Oxford University Press, June 18, 2008), http://dictionary.oed.com/cgi/entry/50134150.

7. Will Eisner, *Graphic Storytelling and Visual Narrative* (Tamarac, FL: Poorhouse Press, 1996), p. 5.

8. Alan Moore, *Writing for Comics*, vol. 1 (Rantoul, IL: Avatar Press, 2007), pp. 3–4.

9. See, for example, chapters 7–10 in Eileen John and Dominic Lopes, eds., *Philosophy of Literature: Contemporary and Classic Readings: An Anthology* (Malden, MA: Blackwell, 2004).

10. The editor and the series editor both accused me of genre snobbery here. I plead not guilty. I'm only reporting what I think other people would say. Really.

11. Also, literature need not be written; look at—or, rather, listen to—oral literature.

12. Monroe Beardsley, "The Concept of Literature," in *Philosophy of Literature: Contemporary and Classic Readings*, p. 57.

13. Terry Eagleton, *Literary Theory: An Introduction* (Minneapolis: University of Minnesota Press, 1983), p. 11.

14. Peter Lamarque and Stein Haugom Olsen, "Literary Practice," in *Philosophy of Literature: Contemporary and Classic Readings*, p. 59.

15. E. D. Hirsch, "What Isn't Literature," in *Philosophy of Literature: Contemporary and Classic Readings*, p. 50.

16. Northrop Frye, *Fearful Symmetry: A Study of William Blake* (Princeton, NJ: Princeton University Press, 1969).

17. For the best discussion of artistic hybridity, see Jerrold Levinson, "Hybrid Art Forms," *Journal of Aesthetic Education* 18 (1984): 5–13.

18. I think this claim is valid, despite the fact that *Watchmen* and many of its kin were published originally as comic book miniseries, since they were clearly designed as coherent, complete wholes. That is, *Watchmen*, *The Dark Knight Returns*, and other true graphic novels do not have the open-ended nature that runs of *Dazzler* or *The Uncanny X-Men* exhibit (even when those latter are packaged as ersatz graphic novels). Think of *Watchmen* as akin to a novel by Charles Dickens, whose great works were originally serialized.

19. For example, in *Understanding Comics: The Invisible Art* (Northampton, MA: Kitchen Sink Press, 1993), Scott McCloud wrote that "it's a mistake to see comics as a mere hybrid of graphic arts and prose fiction. What happens between these panels is a kind of magic only comics can create," p. 92. In McCloud's view, comics have been around for many centuries. But I propose that his timeline is a mistake. Pictorial narrative has been around for centuries—comics are a recent invention. See my "Defining Comics?" *Journal of Aesthetics and Art Criticism* 65 (2007): 369–379.

20. Thanks to Bill Irwin, Rob Loftis, Sheryl Meskin, Stephen Meskin, and Mark White for comments on earlier drafts of this paper.

WATCHWOMEN

Sarah Donovan and Nick Richardson

Readers tend to underestimate the importance of the two Silk Spectres, who seem to get lost in the shuffle of compelling, and perhaps flashier, characters such as Rorschach and the Comedian. But gender issues and the attempted rape have central roles in *Watchmen*, making Sally Jupiter and her daughter, Laurie Juspeczyk, essential characters. To highlight the importance of the *Watchwomen*, let's consider how feminist philosophy can shed light on their role as crime fighters, their provocative costumes, their strained relationship with each other, and the attempted rape of the first Silk Spectre.[1]

She Fights Crime!

As tough women who fight crime on the streets of New York City, both Sally and her daughter are beneficiaries of *liberal feminism*, the mainstream feminist movement of the 1960s in the United States that has its roots in liberal thinkers such as Mary Wollstonecraft (1759–1797) and both John Stuart Mill (1806–1873) and Harriet Taylor Mill (1807–1858). This brand of feminism is based on the liberal political viewpoint that all humans are equal because all humans are rational.[2] If women are rational in the same way that men are, then they deserve the same rights and respect. If women are given the same education and work opportunities that men are given, then women will demonstrate their equality to men.

No stringent social norms or laws prevented Sally and Laurie from pursuing the training necessary to become masked adventurers. The door to equality was opened for them, as envisioned by liberal feminists, and they passed through it. Setting aside the costume and the sexuality of the original Silk Spectre for a moment, we can see Sally as a cut-and-dried liberal feminist. Sally is one of only two female members of the Minutemen, and she is not merely competing with men in a boardroom; she is out there fighting crime on the streets, all the while being a single mother. She is a tough lady competing in a man's world.

We could give a similar liberal feminist interpretation of Laurie's character. Like her mother, she is an unmarried woman, fighting crime alongside her male colleagues. Using a liberal feminist perspective, however, we can argue that Laurie's feminism surpasses her mother's, because Laurie actually seeks to achieve the liberal feminist ideal of androgyny. *Androgyny* is the belief that both men and women have masculine and feminine sides and that if society was more accepting of both social roles, then men and women would be free to develop both sides of their personality, creating a more gender-neutral (and therefore equal) society.

Throughout the story, Laurie is critical of the manner in which her mother utilizes her sexuality to advance her career. Laurie's costume is also sexy (as encouraged by her mother), but, unlike her mother, Laurie does not employ a manager who promotes her as a sex symbol. Ultimately, she decides to change to a more androgynous image. At the end of the graphic novel, after Laurie and Dan Dreiberg become Sandra and Sam Hollis, they discuss a return to adventuring. Laurie says, "'Silk Spectre's' too girly, y'know? Plus, I want a better costume, that protects me: maybe something leather, with a mask over my face. . . . Also, maybe I oughtta carry a gun."[3] Both this new costume and the shift from an early frilly costume to a more practical (and masculine) one mirror the shift undergone by her father, the Comedian, during his career. In true androgynous fashion, Laurie becomes like her father as well as like her mother.

Silk Stockings and Silk Spectres

While Sally's and Laurie's actions may be motivated by liberal feminism, their costumes, Sally's in particular, contradict it. A liberal feminist believes that women and men are equal and that this equality alone is enough for women to achieve what men can achieve. But the original Silk Spectre clearly uses her sexuality and her sexy costume to advance her career. She fully admits this when she says at a Minutemen reunion, "As for me . . . what I achieved . . . sitting in it . . . and as . . . what I achieved it with . . . I'm sitting on it!"[4] A liberal feminist would ask whether the original Silk Spectre is really a feminist insofar as she is working a double standard: she wants equality when it suits her purpose (she fights alongside men), but she wants to play up her femininity and sexuality when it's convenient for her career and her bank account. A liberal feminist does not think that she can have it both ways.

But Laurie's choices about her costume are more complicated and are caught up in her relationship to her mother. Perhaps when Laurie seems to be acting according to the same double standard as her mother, she is simply doing what she is told *by* her mother. Laurie's costume change underscores this interpretation. But this discussion of the costumes can be pushed in a different direction by looking at postmodern feminism's emphasis on the subversive imitation of gender norms.

Postmodern feminism draws on the work of philosophers such as the French feminist Luce Irigaray (1932–present), who uses a point from Jacques Derrida's (1930–2004) method of *deconstruction*. Derrida employed deconstruction to call into question the certainty with which we believe in the reality around us (for example, with regard to our certainty about our gender identities). Derrida underscored the manner in which man and woman have been historically placed in a hierarchical relationship, with man viewed as superior to woman. Derrida tried to deconstruct, or undermine, this as an unchallengeable truth in his own way, but Irigaray's approach will be our focus here.

Irigaray believes that women should exaggerate the stereotypes that surround femininity in order to ultimately challenge those stereotypes, pushing gender stereotypes to their limits to destabilize the hierarchical relationship between man and woman. Irigaray's perspective yields two possible interpretations of Sally's and Laurie's costumes.

The first interpretation is that Sally and Laurie are mimicking stereotypes by dressing in a hypersexualized feminine style while acting out hypermasculine aggressive social behavior. By doing this, they are showing that it is ridiculous to believe that femininity or masculinity is anything other than a social role that we choose to play. Of course, for this interpretation to be true, they would have to engage in this behavior self-consciously, which we are not led to believe that they do.

The second interpretation is that Sally and Laurie only reinforce stereotypes by wearing hypersexualized costumes. In other words, it is acceptable for women to be crime fighters (and thereby take on a masculine social role), but only if their femininity remains beyond question (by their dressing according to a hyperfeminine social role). This interpretation can be pushed further to say that the acceptability of a female crime fighter also depends on her heterosexuality.

Ursula Zandt, aka the Silhouette, was kicked out of the Minutemen when the public discovered that she was a lesbian.

The Silhouette dressed in a feminine manner (although not as hypersexualized as the Silk Spectre), but she transgressed the link between being female, feminine, and heterosexual. Ursula's expulsion from the Minutemen underscores the manner in which society demands that sex, gender, and sexuality all match with what society considers normal.[5] In the end, Sally and Laurie can exist only as second-class citizens in that world. In fact, we can interpret the attempted rape of the first Silk Spectre as evidence for this claim.

No Laughing Matter

The attempted rape plays a complicated role in *Watchmen* in at least three regards. First, and most obviously, it calls into question the image of a hero who is unambiguously on the side of "the good." While Edward Blake, the Comedian, as both rapist and crime fighter is an extreme example, his character underscores an important question in the novel: Who watches the Watchmen? Or, can we trust any human being to have moral authority over another?

Second, the attempted rape shows us something about Sally's relationship, as a woman, to the men in the Minutemen. It demonstrates that she faces a sexist attitude from them that downplays her as a victim. We learn from the actual description of the attempted rape that the Comedian and Hooded Justice react to the situation with blame toward, and indifference to, Sally. Their reactions can be interpreted as a representative sampling of the level of respect that the Minutemen have for Sally as a woman and as a commentary on a very commonly held cultural stereotype about rape.

Moore and Gibbons's account of the attempted rape is violent and depicts Sally as a victim. Sally says that she is going to change from her costume (in an obviously nonsexual context of leaving a photo shoot) and goes to a secluded room for privacy. Blake enters, uninvited. Next, Sally is unambiguous in her rejection of his sexual advance. Rather than leaving, Blake attacks her and tries to rape her while she begs him to leave her alone. Even though Blake insinuates that a woman who dresses like the Silk Spectre must be asking for it, Sally is crystal clear in her rejection of Blake's advances.

Unfortunately, Hooded Justice's verbal response to Sally is indicative of an attitude similar to Blake's. Although he doesn't hesitate to save Sally, he seems to blame her. As she lies on the floor bleeding from the nose, he says nothing more than, "Get up . . . and, for God's sake, cover yourself."[6] Hooded Justice is surprisingly and disappointingly cold, all the more so because we might hope that his internal struggle with sexual orientation would make him more critical of the harmful perception about sex that is influencing his reaction to Sally.[7]

Both the Comedian and Hooded Justice represent the misguided perception that women are responsible for being raped if they dress provocatively. This perception is a sexist attitude that nearly all feminists would reject, insofar as it follows a warped logic that is disrespectful of men as well as of women. For women, it suggests that a woman's style of dress trumps her rational, verbal ability to give or deny sexual consent (the dangerous belief that "she wanted it" or that "no means yes"). For men, it suggests both that men cannot distinguish between style of dress and explicit sexual consent, and that men cannot control themselves in the presence of a scantily clad woman. Sadly enough, it is an attitude that Sally herself has perhaps internalized (and this is, of course, complicated by her subsequent consensual sexual relationship with Blake). Later, Sally is asked in an interview about the attempted rape, and she expresses an ambiguous attitude:

> You know, rape is rape and there's no excuses for it, absolutely none, but for me, I felt . . . I felt like I'd contributed in some way. Is that misplaced guilt, whatever my analyst said? I really felt that, that I was somehow

as much to blame for . . . for letting myself be his victim not in a physical sense, but . . . but, it's like what if, y'know? What if, just for a moment, maybe I really did want . . . I mean, that doesn't excuse him, doesn't excuse either of us, but with all that doubt, what it is to come to terms with it, I can't stay angry when I'm so uncertain about my own feelings.[8]

Sally seems to have internalized an opinion about rape that slides too easily and uncritically from an acknowledgment of physical attraction on her part to an acceptance of blame, despite the clear fact that attempted rape is physical violence and brutality.

The third aspect of the attempted rape raises the complicated issue about Sally eventually consenting to sex with a man who tried to rape her. How could she bring herself to do this? Rather than offer a feminist justification or condemnation of Sally's actions, it is actually in line with the graphic novel itself not to resolve this question. The whole point of that storyline is that it resists interpretation according to any theory—it is utterly too messy and complex. The attempted rape, the subsequent consensual relationship, and Laurie as the end product of it are meant to sit side by side in the graphic novel in an unresolved fashion.

Dr. Manhattan best captures the meaning of this uncomfortable sequence, and its resistance to any theory that could make sense of it, when he sees the beauty in the horror of Laurie's realization that Blake is her father:

Thermodynamic miracles . . . events with odds against so astronomical they're effectively impossible, like oxygen spontaneously becoming gold. I long to observe such a thing. And yet, in each human coupling, a thousand million sperm vie for a single egg. Multiply those odds by countless generations, against the odds of your ancestors being alive; meeting; siring this precise son;

that exact daughter . . . until your mother loves a man she has every reason to hate, and of that union, of the thousand million children competing for fertilization, it was you, only you, that emerged. To distill so specific a form from that chaos of improbability, like turning air to gold . . . that is the crowning unlikelihood. The thermodynamic miracle.[9]

Dr. Manhattan's comments are appropriate because he recognizes that what Blake did was wrong, that Sally has every right to hate him, but that for one afternoon she did not, and Laurie—whom he loves—was the result of Sally's ambiguous feelings about Blake. As Dr. Manhattan gracefully captures it, this is the kind of chaos that eludes theory.

Mommy Dearest?

The relationship between Sally and Laurie allows us to examine another branch of feminist theory, *existential feminism*. Laurie is very critical of her mother as a person and of her mother's choices when she was a member of the Minutemen. Two examples underscore this. First, when we initially meet Laurie, she rejects Rorschach's greeting of her as "Miss Jupiter": "That's Juspeczyk. 'Jupiter' was just a name my mother assumed because she didn't want anyone to know she was Polish."[10] Second, when Laurie visits her mother in California, while the Comedian's funeral is taking place in New York, Sally shows Laurie a pornographic comic, based on the original Silk Spectre, that a male fan sent to Sally. Sally conveys to Laurie that she finds it flattering, and her daughter's response is very critical: "Mother, this is vile! I just, jeez, I just don't know how you can stand being degraded like this. I mean, don't you care how people see you?" When her mother does not respond, Laurie continues, "I said, doesn't this sleazeball image bother you? Honestly, mother, you . . ."[11] Sally cuts off her daughter with a comment that indicates she finds Laurie's words idealistic and naive. She retaliates by ridiculing Laurie for the public image that she has cultivated when she says, "At least I don't sleep with an H-bomb."[12] In fact, it seems like the only thing that endears Sally to Laurie is Laurie's knowledge of the Comedian's attempted rape of her mother.

The existential feminism of Simone de Beauvoir (1908–1986) can shed light on this troubled relationship. Central to existentialism is self-definition and the awareness of one's condition as undefined in any metaphysical sense. We are not born with the blueprint of who we must become; there is nothing that absolutely determines the course of one's life (although we certainly have to take one's historical and material circumstances into account when we think of what is possible). The existentialist Jean-Paul Sartre (1905–1980), who also happens to have been the life partner of Simone de Beauvoir, distinguished between our human condition, which is that we are "condemned to be free," and the various roles that we play in life. Sartre urged us not to confuse the roles that we play with an "essence." We play all sorts of roles throughout our lives (such as student, friend, brother, sister, employee) but we should never forget that, in the end, we are not these roles in any deep sense—we are free to act in any way we choose. When we insist that we *are* any one role we play (in the sense that we had no choice), then we are denying our freedom. For Sartre, this denial of freedom is a form of lying to oneself that he calls "bad faith." We are also in bad faith when we do not take responsibility for defining ourselves; for example, if we blame our life circumstances on others or on chance, instead of understanding how we contribute to them.

Beauvoir draws on existentialist theory in her famous book *The Second Sex* to oppose *biological essentialism*, the belief that biology determines your social behavior. According to Beauvoir, not only is no one determined by an inherent essence such as rationality, one's anatomy also does not determine one's social behavior. As she famously stated in *The Second Sex*, "One is not born, but rather becomes a woman."[13] Expanding this, using the language of *transcendence* to describe a person who actively pursues his or her projects and *immanence* for a person who allows himself or herself to be defined, Beauvoir discusses how this distinction falls along gender lines. Women tend to be more passive (or immanent) with regard to life, and men tend to be more active (or transcendent). Although this may be descriptively correct (and keep in mind that she wrote this in the 1940s), according to an existentialist perspective, there is no essence inherent to men or women that determines their social behavior. Women can be just as active as men, and men can be just as passive as women.

Sally is an existential feminist, insofar as she chose her own path in life by becoming the original Silk Spectre. Since it was a rather daring path, it is unlikely that she felt pressured to choose it out of obedience to social norms. While Sally demonstrates some qualities of an existential feminist, Laurie is clearly in bad faith throughout most of the story because she assumes a position of immanence and allows others to define her.[14] In other words, she does not recognize her existential freedom, and, furthermore, Laurie's bad faith complicates her relationship with her mother.

Three examples show how Laurie is in a position of immanence from which she allows everyone around her to define her. First, Sally groomed Laurie from a young age to be a masked adventurer. As an adult, Laurie recognizes that it was never her choice. After Laurie leaves Dr. Manhattan and begins staying at Dan (Nite Owl) Dreiberg's house, she and Dan express regrets about their choice to be masked adventurers. Laurie says in response to his claim that his choice was a childish fantasy, "Yeah, well at least you were living out your own fantasies. I was living out my mother's."[15]

Second, at just sixteen years of age, Laurie was dating Dr. Manhattan and fighting crime. From an existentialist perspective, we could say that Laurie moved from allowing her mother to define her to allowing Dr. Manhattan to define her. As an example, when Laurie goes out to dinner with Dan early in the book, she jokes sarcastically that she is a "kept woman" on the military base. She tells Dan her regrets about her life when she says, "It's just I keep thinking 'I'm thirty-five. What have I done?' I've spent eight years in semi-retirement, preceded by ten years running round in a stupid costume because my stupid mother wanted me to! You remember that costume? With that stupid little short skirt and the neckline going down to my navel? God that was so dreadful."[16] And as she describes in a conversation with Dan, she realizes that she was allowed to live on the military base only because the government needed her to keep Dr. Manhattan happy.

Third, she moves directly from her relationship with Dr. Manhattan to her relationship with Dan. Her entire life is marked by a pattern of aligning herself with others who will define her. We could argue, however, that at the end of the novel, Laurie becomes more of an existential feminist, a change marked by a new name and a change of appearance so drastic that her own mother does not recognize her. Furthermore, she talks about designing her own costume. These may be markers that Laurie has finally declared independence from her mother and is at last defining herself.

We Leave It Entirely in Your Hands

As we've seen, feminist philosophy contains a diversity of perspectives, only a few of which we have considered here. And looking at the crime-fighting careers of Sally and Laurie can lead us back to the real world. For example, we can apply feminist principles in terms of how we think about jobs that our society has labeled "masculine" or "feminine." How do we think about female police officers, soldiers, doctors, CEOs, and presidential hopefuls? Conversely, how do we view male kindergarten teachers, daycare providers, nurses, flight attendants, and stay-at-home dads? Do we still have stereotypes about masculine and feminine social behavior that limit individual potential and choice? What would it take as a society to rid us of our gender stereotypes, and do people want this? And could studying *Watchmen* help?

NOTES

1. A great text to introduce readers to the diversity of feminist philosophy is Rosemary Putnam Tong's *Feminist Thought: A More Comprehensive Introduction*, 2nd ed. (Boulder, CO: Westview, 1998). The general classifications we use here (liberal feminism, postmodern feminism, and existential feminism) are explained in much greater depth with a wider range of authors in Tong's text.

2. This can be extended so that by virtue of being rational, as argued by Enlightenment philosopher Immanuel Kant (1724–1804), we all have an intrinsic worth and are deserving of respect.

3. *Watchmen*, chap. XII, p. 30.

4. Ibid., chap. IX, p. 11.

5. Feminist philosophy certainly discusses sexuality; Judith Butler's 1990 text *Gender Trouble: Feminism and the Subversion of Identity* (New York: Routledge, 2006) is a well-known treatment of both feminism and homosexuality. (Butler is also often classified under "queer theory." Queer theory encompasses feminist issues, as well as gay, lesbian, bisexual, transgender, and intersexed issues.)

6. *Watchmen*, chap. II, p. 8.

7. For more on Hooded Justice's homosexuality, see chapter 14 in this book, "Hooded Justice and Captain Metropolis: The Ambiguously Gay Duo," by Rob Arp.

8. *Watchmen*, chap. IX, supplemental material, excerpt from "Probe Profile: Sally Jupiter," September 1976, p. 22.

9. Ibid., chap. IX, pp. 26–27.

10. Ibid., chap. I, p. 20.

11. Ibid., chap. II, p. 8.

12. Ibid.

13. Simone de Beauvoir, *The Second Sex*, trans. and ed. H. M. Parshley (1952; repr., New York: Vintage Books, 1989), p. 267.

14. Although, if we examine Sally's conversations with her adult daughter, she seems unable to embrace her life as an older woman. This indicates that she is clinging to the image of who she was in her youth. This is a sign of bad faith setting in during her golden years; bad faith in this context is unwillingness to see that one is condemned to freedom. By longing for the past, Sally is missing out on the present.

15. *Watchmen*, chap. VII, p. 5.

16. Ibid., chap. I, p. 25.

HOODED JUSTICE AND CAPTAIN METROPOLIS: THE AMBIGUOUSLY GAY DUO

Robert Arp

We don't talk about it much, and we may be ashamed of it, but some of us (especially guys) are shocked and bothered when we find out some people (again, especially guys) are gay. We can accept that the hairstylist or the Broadway dancer or George Michael is gay. But we can't accept it so easily when it's revealed that our favorite football player or perhaps even one of our close friends is gay. I wasn't *really* surprised when Rob Halford of Judas Priest came out of the closet, but it did make me feel a bit uncomfortable about the posters I had on my bedroom wall during high school. Halford was supposed to be a "real man," but like many guys, I made the mistake of thinking "real men" are heterosexual. That's part of what's so jarring about *Brokeback Mountain*: these are supposed to be cowboys! Superheroes are also stereotypically hypermasculine "real men." That's why it's hard to accept that Hooded Justice and

Captain Metropolis may be gay. Superheroes, football players, rock stars, and cowboys can kick your ass, so we feel somehow emasculated in realizing they're gay.

I have to admit that when I first read about Hooded Justice and Captain Metropolis, I said, "Oh, no," and closed the book. I have a visceral negative reaction to the thought of another man looking at me with desire or "wanting me," and I'm basically uncomfortable with the gay lifestyle. But I'm uncomfortable with a lot of other things that, when I think about them, I don't go off half-cocked (no pun intended) about. So what makes homosexuality so different?

"Those People" Are Unnatural

How many times have we heard *this* claim!? The idea is simple: since most people on the planet are oriented to a heterosexual lifestyle, complete with heterosexual desires, sex, relationships, public ceremonies, housing, and the like, this is *the* natural way of things, period. Any deviation from this natural, heterosexual lifestyle is unnatural, almost by definition. Thus, homosexuality is unnatural.[1] I assume most people in the *Watchmen* alternative universe would likely agree with this, too.

To make sense of this attitude, we need to distinguish between homosexual *orientation* and homosexual *action*. Let's say that *orientation* refers to the basic, primal, instinctive kinds of desires and wants of someone's personality that, at present, makes that person either a homosexual (HM) or a heterosexual (HT). On the other hand, *action* refers to the acts and the behaviors that may stem from an orientation.

There are tests that one can take to see whether one is oriented to be an HM or an HT. For example, answer these questions:

• Do you get sexually aroused at the thought of having sexual contact of any kind with someone of the same sex?

- Can you see yourself in an intimate relationship sharing the deepest parts of your life with someone of the same sex?

If you answered yes to these questions, you're likely an HM. There are other questions that can be asked to get at someone's real orientation, but you get the picture.[2] So, regardless of the way someone acts, looks, or sounds on the outside, he may still be an HM on the inside in terms of his basic orientation. After all, if it's true that Captain Metropolis and Hooded Justice are gay, they sure as heck don't *act* and *look* like they are gay. They don't (publicly) display any *actions* associated with their *orientation*—otherwise, the revelation wouldn't be as surprising.

Notice that in an earlier paragraph, I said, "at present," which could be taken to mean that one's orientation can change. Some people think that you choose your orientation.[3] Studies confirm that HM orientation is present in childhood, however, long before a person has enough life experience to make a fully conscious, rational choice of orientation.[4] Brain and genetic studies support this gay-by-nature, or "gayture," hypothesis.[5] Experience also bears this out. The HMs I have known all tell me they have had these feelings, thoughts, and beliefs since early childhood.

In fact, it's absurd to think that people choose to be gay. Would you choose to be the outcast of every society? Would you choose to be "locked in the closet" or come out of the closet to be ridiculed, harassed, and perhaps even killed, by the HT majority? Would you choose to have Silk Spectre on your arm, knowing that it was all a lie and for show? Would you choose to have every friend you had on Wednesday, December 31, 1999, desert you and shun you on Thursday, January 1, 2000, after you out yourself at the Millennium party the night before? I doubt it. I can no more help the fact that I am a red-blooded American HT than Nathan Lane can help that he is a red-blooded American HM.

So, are HMs unnatural in their orientation? If what we mean by unnatural is *abnormal*, and what we mean by abnormal is *not in the majority*, then yes: HMs are unnatural just as left-handed people are. By various counts—depending on males versus females, city versus rural areas, and other factors—somewhere between 5 and 15 percent of the world's population are HM, although, lately it seems like the number is higher, with the amount of celebrity HMs who have come out of the closet.[6] This kind of "unnatural" really isn't unnatural at all, though, and it certainly is nothing to blame anyone for or be ashamed of.

But a different understanding of "unnatural" implies that HMs are disordered or evil, as if they had a disease of some kind.[7] Should we think that HMs are unnatural in this evil way? Plenty of HMs I know are very kind, generous, and gifted; the world would definitely suffer for their loss. Just consider the number of comic books, graphic novels, and other creative media that would not exist.[8] Plus, during my experience while studying to be a Catholic priest for nine years, I found that gays make the most sensitive pastoral ministers, especially at the most difficult times—for example, when death or illness overtakes us. Furthermore, there are plenty of geniuses throughout Western history who were supposedly gay, likely gay, or confirmed gay, such as Socrates, Michelangelo, Oscar Wilde, Alan Turing, Ludwig Wittgenstein, Elton John, and many others.[9] A lot of gays today are geniuses of one kind or another, but we wouldn't know it because of the stigma that forces them to stay in the closet.

The "Tab A Fits into Slot A" Argument

"Sure," says the proponent of this naturalist view, "but HMs can't breed the way HTs can, and so they're unnatural! It's natural for man to breed with woman, and since man on man or woman on woman couplings never can lead to breeding,

HMs are unnatural." Let's call this line of thinking the *ideal view of natural processes*, in which every part and process associated with human anatomy and physiology is functioning the ideally correct way. This line of thinking has obvious flaws, such as making a lot of HTs out to be unnatural: a barren HT woman and an HT man who shoots blanks would also be considered unnatural because their natural parts aren't functioning ideally. "True," says the naturalist who holds to this ideal view of natural processes, "and the cold hard fact is that the barren HT woman and the HT man shooting blanks *are* unnatural, because their parts aren't functioning in a natural fashion."

Okay, but then we're back to the majority-equals-natural argument, which, interestingly enough, makes most people out to be unnatural, abnormal freaks because almost no one has an ideal human anatomy and physiology! Virtually everyone has some quirk, problem, malfunction, part missing, or part not working properly that makes him or her *unnatural*, according to this view. My uncle John is a disordered aberration; he's been missing a finger since birth! Einstein, too, that weirdo—a section of his brain was too large in relation to other people's brains! And my wife, the cancer survivor, is using her stomach as her esophagus: disgusting freak of nature! And me with my vasectomy, forget it, I'm a monstrosity!

So, what's actually natural is just the way things are in the biological, chemical, and physical worlds, with all of the screwed-up, disordered monstrosities and flaws (compared to the ideal view of natural processes). If we are going to stick with categorizing the orientation of people as natural, we should think of HMs as natural, but merely *different* from HTs. So, both HMs and HTs *are* natural, they're simply two different kinds of natural, like lefthanders and righthanders, and there may even be more natural kinds, such as bisexuals and ambidextrous people.

Homosexuals are often victimized by the "ick" factor: we assume that just because being gay is "icky" to so many people, then it must be disordered. But this doesn't follow logically, and it doesn't apply to a lot of other things. Think of a standard mammalian birth, with all of the juices, blood, and afterbirth. That's totally disgusting and icky to most people, but we would never condemn it as unnatural. The same goes for any number of icky processes, activities, behaviors, and what not.

So, the least we should do is *investigate* more what the icky process, activity, or behavior is before judging it, and lots of people *don't* do that with HMs. In fact:

- HMs don't necessarily spread diseases such as AIDS.
- HMs aren't always thinking about sex (despite the fact that the newspaperman in *Watchmen* chapter III thinks that just because a man and a woman can't relate sexually, then the man must be "queer as a three-dollar bill").
- HMs aren't likely to be child molesters.
- HMs aren't necessarily cross-dressers or transvestites (not that there's anything wrong with that).
- Not all HMs like anal penetration (one of my gay friends tried it once and will never do it again).
- Not all HMs like rough sex or "get hot" because of male beatings (I'm thinking of Eddie Blake's comments to Hooded Justice, while Justice is beating Blake's ass to save Silk Spectre from getting raped by Blake in *Watchmen*, chapter II).
- Many HMs are spiritual and religious.
- Not all male HMs are effeminate (Hooded Justice, Captain Metropolis, Rock Hudson), and not all female HMs are butch (Silhouette, the female characters in *Chasing Amy* and *Kissing Jessica Stein*).
- HMs are not always looking at members of the same sex to "try to pick them up" or convert them.

Perhaps if these things were more widely known, the ick factor would go down, or at least people would realize that it's their problem, not the HMs'.

They Act Out on Their
Screwed-Up Desires

One could maintain that HMs can't help it, but they're still unnatural in their orientation the same way that pedophiles and other deviants are. We all think that pedophiles have an unnatural orientation and desire for children. Here we need to consider homosexual *action* versus orientation. You can be oriented one way, but your actions are a different story altogether. Even if HMs and pedophiles are naturally oriented, one could argue that they still both need to be stopped. We need to medicate and counsel them or, as a last resort, cut their testicles off so that they can't act upon their orientations. Or, they just need to stay ambiguously gay and in the closet like Captain Metropolis and Hooded Justice—and *never* act out.

HMs are, however, quite distinct from pedophiles. The actions of pedophiles in molesting children are, by their very nature, harmful to others, but not so the actions of HMs. Why do we think that the pedophile's act is immoral or wrong? Because the pedophile's action in molesting the child is harmful to the child, period.[10] And according to some moral rule that says, "It is immoral to do what is deliberately harmful," the pedophile acts immorally. There is no such thing as a good, right, or moral act of child molestation. We can't say this, necessarily, for the HM, because there are such things as good, right, or moral HM acts; not every HM act need be evil.

Let's go right to the meat of the matter and consider the HM sexual act. It seems to me that it is possible for an HM to be in an intimate, healthy sexual relationship with another HM, with both people fully rational, both fully taking responsibility for their actions, and both *not* trying to give the other person AIDS or some social disease. Why does the HM sexual act automatically signal an *immoral* act? What's interesting is that two HTs can be in a relationship based purely on sex, drugs, and rock 'n' roll, and most people would still see that as less morally problematic than two HMs involved in a twelve-year loving relationship out in the suburbs.

Here, the proponent of what's natural could step forward and note that "ideally, according to the *natural view of natural activities*, sex should be between a man and a woman and should be open to the possibility of procreation. After all, this is what such a natural activity ideally leads to." The person may even say something further like this: "Any other kind of sexual interaction is unnatural and, hence, immoral." Yet this line of thinking has obvious flaws, such as making a lot of HTs out to be immoral. Lots of HTs can't procreate, for one reason or another, yet they still engage in sexual intercourse, and we wouldn't want them not to engage in sex just because they can't procreate, would we? Those evil barren daughters and blank-shooting sons of bitches! How dare they attempt to have sex for something like *love* or *intimacy*! Do we really want to say that barren women and blank-shooters are immoral when they have sex?

Furthermore, this natural view of natural activities leads to the idea that just because *it is* the case (sex leads to breeding) means that *it ought to be* the case (sex ought to always lead to breeding). Now, just because something is the case does not mean that it ought to be the case; just because *it is* the case that I want five pieces of cake or don't want to take the final exam, doesn't mean that I *ought to* eat the cake or not take the exam, right? So, there's a problem with this kind of thinking. Just because, *ideally*, sex leads to breeding doesn't mean that it ought to or that sex that doesn't lead to breeding is wrong.

If we did follow this "is-therefore-ought" line of reasoning all the way, we'd arrive at the following insight: it *is* the case that a certain percentage of humans and other animals perform gay acts; therefore, they *ought to* perform gay acts![11] So, I don't see what all the fuss is about from these "natural view of natural activities" types, given their is-therefore-ought position.

It clearly is the case that gays around the world are doing gay things; hence, it ought to be that we allow them to do their gay things and leave them alone!

Okay, but Don't Allow 'Em to Marry Each Other!

If most people are HTs, and lots of HTs are icked out by HMs, then we can see why HTs deny HMs many rights and privileges. So if you're gay, chances are you're not going to be able to get married or benefit from your partner's health insurance plan, in addition to many other things.[12] This is another reason that, most likely, *Watchmen*'s ambiguously gay duo stayed in the closet.

Why are HTs so opposed to gay marriage? Well, first off, some people want to call it a "civil union" instead, arguing that the term *marriage* means, by definition, "a bond between a man and a woman that leads to children." So HMs can feel free to form civil unions, but they can't ever get married, by definition. Of course, these same people then want to say that the rights and the privileges afforded to marriages should not be afforded to unions. Since a union is just a name with no real social backing or benefits, the HMs lose. Furthermore, marriages where people are not open to or able to have children aren't really marriages either, by this definition, which seems crazy. Despite the license, church ceremony, wedding vows, years together, intimacy, commitment, trust, loyalty, and what not, a large number of my friends, then, are not married!

A popular argument against allowing HMs to marry is that if we allow a man to marry a man or a woman to marry a woman, then the next thing you know we'll be allowing men to marry their dogs and women to marry their horses. Therefore, we can't allow HMs to marry. This is called a "slippery slope argument"—allowing gay marriage, by this logic, would start us on a slippery slope leading to marriage involving animals (or children or multiple partners). But it does not necessarily follow that marrying someone of the same sex will lead to cross-species marriages. Just because a guy wants to marry a guy does not mean the same guy will want to marry his pet hamster. And furthermore, we can easily enact laws that say men can marry men, but men can't marry hamsters. (And since hamsters don't have the legal capacity to enter into contracts—until the Ninth Circuit Court of Appeals has a killer acid trip—this law should be easy to pass!)

Another reason people say that HMs should not marry has to do with the screwed-up families that would be produced or the way that the kids from HM families turn out to be screwed up themselves, by either turning gay, doing drugs, or becoming underachievers. But there is no indication that HM families are any more or less dysfunctional than HT families are, all things considered.[13] And with respect to any data that indicate that kids from HM families are screwed up, I have this to say: because kids from HM families must deal with the added social stigma of coming from such an environment, *of course* they're going to wind up a little bit screwed up. Until the rest of the world accepts HMs and does not discriminate against, laugh at, ridicule, and/or harm them, the kids of HMs will be dealing with a lot of extra crap that kids from HT families don't have to deal with.

Should They All Be Rounded Up?

In the name of Captain Metropolis and Hooded Justice, *no*, HMs should not all be rounded up! Currently, HMs are treated as second-class citizens with partial rights and privileges, much as blacks were in the past. The gay rights movement of today, much like the civil rights movement of the 1960s, will likely bring about recognition and validation of HMs as full members of our society and others. States are starting to wise up and allow gays to get married, paving the way for this recognition.

Most of the problem has to do with not getting to know your HM family members, friends, and neighbors. So, maybe we should "round 'em all up," or at least some of them, so that we can pick their brains, have coffee, share experiences, and go shopping for shoes. Speaking of shoes, if we HTs could spend a little time in the shoes of HMs, then maybe we would grant them the same kinds of rights, privileges and, above all, *respect* that we HTs share. Maybe we would find that like Captain Metropolis and Hooded Justice in *Watchmen*, a lot of these HMs are actually heroes.

NOTES

1. A basic example, which is a fairly common belief in all of the world's major religions and of the majority of the world (it seems), is this statement from the Catholic Church: "Basing itself on sacred Scripture, which presents homosexual acts as acts of grave depravity, tradition has always declared that homosexual acts are intrinsically disordered. They are contrary to the natural law. They close the sexual act to the gift of life. They do not proceed from a genuine affective and sexual complementarity. Under no circumstances can they be approved" (*The Catechism of the Catholic Church*, paragraph 2357).

2. S. Brady and W. J. Busse, "The Gay Identity Questionnaire: A Brief Measure of Homosexual Identity Formation," *Journal of Homosexuality* 26 (1994): 1–22.

3. See, for example, Joseph Nicolosi and Linda Nicolosi, *A Parent's Guide to Preventing Homosexuality* (Downer's Grove, IL: InterVarsity Press, 2002).

4. Eric Marcus, *Is It a Choice? Answers to 300 of the Most Frequently Asked Questions about Gays and Lesbians* (San Francisco, CA: Harper, 1993); Neil Risch, Elizabeth Squires-Wheeler, and Bronya Keats, "Male Sexual Orientation and Genetic Evidence," *Science* 262 (1993) 2063–2064.

5. Simon LeVay, "A Difference in Hypothalamic Structure between Heterosexual and Homosexual Men," *Science* 253 (1991): 1034–1037; Dean Hamer et al., "A Linkage between DNA Markers on the X Chromosome and Male Sexual Orientation," *Science* 261 (1993): 321–327.

6. Preeti Pathela et al., "Discordance between Sexual Behavior and Self-Reported Sexual Identity: A Population-Based Survey of New York City Men," *Annals of Internal Medicine* 145 (2006): 416–425.

7. For years, psychologists considered homosexuality to be disordered but have reconsidered this label. See Irving Bieber, "On Arriving at the American Psychiatric Association Decision on Homosexuality," *NARTH Bulletin* 7 (1999): 15–23.

8. For example, Joe Phillips is an openly gay comic book illustrator who has worked for DC Comics and Innovation Comics. See http://en.wikipedia.org/wiki/Joe_Phillips. And there are plenty of others: Allan Heinberg, Phil Jimenez, and more.

9. See Thomas Cowan, *Gay Men and Women Who Enriched the World* (Boston: Alyson Publications, 1992), and the articles in Martin Duberman, Martha Vicinus, and George Chauncey, eds., *Hidden from History: Reclaiming the Gay and Lesbian Past* (New York: Meridian, 1990).

10. See, for example, S. Mihailides, G. Devilly, and T. Ward, "Implicit Cognitive Distortions and Sexual Offending," *Sex Abuse* 16 (2004): 333–350.

11. See, for example, Bruce Bagemihl, *Biological Exuberance: Animal Homosexuality and Natural Diversity* (New York: St. Martin's Press, 2000).

12. For a list of the hundreds of rights and privileges HTs have that HMs don't have, see the Human Rights Campaign Web site, www.hrc.org/, and www.speakout .com/activism/gayrights/.

13. There are tons of these studies, but see, for example, N. Anderssen, C. Amlie, and E. Ytteroy, "Outcomes for Children with Lesbian or Gay Parents: A Review of Studies from 1978 to 2000," *Scandinavian Journal of Psychology* 43 (2002): 335–351.

WHAT'S SO GODDAMNED FUNNY? THE COMEDIAN AND RORSCHACH ON LIFE'S WAY

Taneli Kukkonen

Living in the world of *Watchmen* is no laughing matter. Random, brutal violence rules the streets, while the specter of nuclear apocalypse looms ever larger. Faced with such gloomy prospects, costumed adventurers as well as ordinary citizens end up feeling bitter, alienated, and powerless. Still, the "masks," as Rorschach calls them, assiduously cling to their assumed roles, each following his or her chosen path. Some even choose to emphasize the lighter side of life, notably Eddie Blake, the Comedian, whose murder drives the *Watchmen* narrative. But is there philosophical meaning in the Comedian's laughter? That's the issue we'll explore in this chapter (no joke).

Understanding the Self: The Veidt Method

Philosophers generally are not known for their sense of humor (no, seriously!). A notable exception is the Danish thinker

Søren Kierkegaard (1813–1855), who not only exhibits a fine comic sensibility in his writings but also has a theory of humor every bit as subtle as his jokes.

Kierkegaard has variously been called the father, the forefather, and the godfather of the philosophical movement known as *existentialism*. Typical of existentialism is an emphasis on the individual subject as the focus of all philosophy, as well as the claim that we are each responsible for what we make of ourselves—the Veidt outlook and the Veidt method in action, one might say. "Perhaps I decided to be intelligent rather than otherwise? Perhaps we all make such decisions, though that seems a callous doctrine."[1] As for Kierkegaard, he explains his understanding of existence in the following manner: "There are three existence-spheres: the esthetic, the ethical, the religious. The metaphysical is abstraction, and there is no human being who exists metaphysically. The metaphysical, the ontological, *is*, but it does not *exist*, for when it exists it does so in the esthetic, in the ethical, in the religious."[2]

Central here is the contention that philosophy strays from its calling whenever it seeks to answer general questions about the world in a supposedly detached and objective manner. To Kierkegaard, this would be an indicator that *metaphysics*, which fancies itself the study of *being* in the universal sense, has suppressed the all-important questions that the subject must set for himself or herself as a living, breathing person. "Thus abstract thinking helps me with my immortality by killing me as a particular existing individual and then making me immortal, and therefore helps somewhat as in Holberg the doctor took the patient's life with his medicine—but also drove out the fever."[3] The metaphysical approach, however, does not work, because as the existentialist par excellence Jean-Paul Sartre said, "Existence precedes essence." Choosing a life may very well prove distressing (Sartre spoke of nausea), but it cannot be sidestepped by cravenly referring to some off-the-peg model of being to which one *must* subscribe. There simply is no such necessity in human life.[4]

For Kierkegaard, too, life is meant to be a feverish, passionate business. The lofty speculations of the metaphysicians are just that—speculation—and it is therefore on existence that philosophers should focus their sights: "The subjective thinker's task is to *understand himself in existence.*"[5] Furthermore, for Kierkegaard, nobody can have a complete and synoptic picture of the different lives available to individual humans. "Consequently, *(a) a logical system can be given; (b) but a system of existence cannot be given.*"[6] Among other things, this means that there is no way to compare ways of life except by passing through them. As Aristotle had already observed, in life, as in the Olympic Games, it is not the armchair experts on the sidelines who are rewarded, or even those who might be the strongest and the most beautiful, but those who actually compete.[7] In Kierkegaard's eyes, this would be a peculiar strength of all of *Watchmen*'s masked heroes, even the most muddled and immoral: at one time or another, they have all put their very selves on the line. The costumed heroes, through the act of putting on those costumes, have become something more than daydreamers: they have begun to *exist.*[8]

Worms in the Apple

Humor takes its start from questioning, doubt, and even open ridicule. Where, then, does it fall among Kierkegaard's esthetic, ethical, and religious stages of existence? The short answer is: between the cracks. Laughter signals transcendence; it indicates that a person has realized the limits of a particular viewpoint, even as some attachment to that same viewpoint still remains. (After all, if the person had genuinely moved on, he or she would no longer be dwelling on the outlook now being ridiculed. A negative obsession is still an obsession.)

For some people, the desire to put things in their place becomes an end in itself. Hence, the Comedian's motto: "I keep things in proportion an' try ta see the funny side."[9]

This corresponds to Kierkegaard's understanding of *irony*.
According to Kierkegaard, people rarely have the ability to put
their own views or lifestyles into perspective, and that *finitude*
is grist for the ironist's mill. Kierkegaard's notion is, of course,
a far cry from the dictionary definition of irony, which hinges
on somebody saying one thing while intending the opposite.
("Nice jacket.") Verbal irony for Kierkegaard is fine as far as
it goes, but, true to his existentialist leanings, Kierkegaard
insists that the consummate ironist would apply the same
approach to his very life, conducting himself in a certain manner while inwardly not believing in the ideals he superficially
espouss. Compare this again to Eddie Blake. Eddie's chosen
name as an adventurer is the Comedian, and yet much of what
he has to say doesn't seem all that funny. He poses as a hero,
and yet his behavior is anything but heroic. Eddie is a murderer, a rapist, and a thug, and yet he seems to be at ease in the
corridors of power. To accomplish this, one must be quite a
skilled ironist. How does Eddie do it, and why?

Essential to the ironist's stance is the notion that life is a game
and that only mugs and losers take it too seriously.[10] The ironist
believes in his own superiority: he alone has all of the answers,
he alone can see through the charade, while the rest of the
world is blind. "What's going down in this world, you got no
idea. Believe me," Eddie says.[11] The Comedian believes that
all the world's a stage for fools who think they're playing at
being heroes, which is consistent with Kierkegaard's description of comedy. In comedy, the characters in the play think that
they're being heroic, while the outside spectator perceives the
ridiculousness of such pretenses. This is what gives a story its
comic effect:

> In it there must not be a single character, not a single
> stage situation, that could claim to survive the downfall
> that irony from the outset prepares for each and all
> in it. When the curtain falls, everything is forgotten,

nothing but nothing remains, and that is the only thing one sees; and the only thing one hears is a laughter, like a sound of nature, that does not issue from any one person but is the language of a world force, and this force is irony.[12]

The ironist's burden is to annihilate any meaning in the world, for to allow the possibility of any true heroism or any real tragedy would be to admit that the ironist's superior, belittling judgment does not, after all, reach everywhere. This would amount to taking irony ironically, which is an impossible, self-effacing move.[13]

Still, life's comedy can be black indeed, as Veidt acknowledges.[14] When challenged to find something funny in charred villages and necklaces made out of human ears, Eddie has to drop his pretence. The ironist doesn't know anything more than anyone else does—he's just learned to play a different game. "Hey . . . I never said it was a good joke! I'm just playin' along with the gag."[15] This is the ironist's trap: he can only ever "play along," never create anything of independent value. Irony by definition is a parasitic entity, feeding off other, more serious, opinions and activities.

Consider furthermore the dynamic between the ironist and his audience. We would expect a comedian (and *the* Comedian) to want to elicit a few laughs every now and then for the sake of easy gratification. Eddie does stoop to explaining his jokes from time to time, such as when the Crimebusters' one and only meeting gets deflated by a single well-timed burp.[16] But by letting his audience in on his insights, the ironist annuls the distance between others and himself. This is antithetical to the very movement of irony, which hinges on a distinction between the hapless, sincere outsider and the cynical insider. Consequently, Eddie prefers to keep his audience mostly in the dark.[17]

In one extreme example, Eddie plays an astonishing triple feint when asked about the death of the Watergate reporters in *Watchmen*'s past. "Nah . . . I'm clean, guys. Just don't ask where I was when I heard about J.F.K."[18] Everybody laughs, thinking that they're in on the joke, but in reality the joke is on them. As we learn later, Blake really *did* kill Kennedy, and in all likelihood he murdered Woodward and Bernstein too.[19] It is befitting of the supreme ironist to hide in plain sight like this. Blake admits by denying, at the same time that he denies by admitting, thereby leading his audience to believe that they should annul the tacit admission and believe in his innocence after all. By allowing his audience in on part of the joke, the Comedian gets to keep the rest for himself and ensures that his superiority is maintained at all times. This is a dizzying hall of mirrors, but it is only in such games that the ironist can lose himself and the dread constantly nipping at his heels. "He always thought he'd get the last laugh," Sally Jupiter says about Eddie in a rare moment of clarity.[20]

In the End, a Man Stands Alone

The ironist's victory ultimately rings hollow. He can never look himself in the eye, nor can he ever take a single thing seriously. For example, Eddie Blake is denied a place in any serious relationship or family life. To Kierkegaard, such domesticity is the paradigm of the ethical mode of existence, the next step on the existential ladder—not flashy, perhaps, but full of meaningful instances of sharing and caring. In recognizing and fulfilling mutual duties, people attain a quiet satisfaction from living the ethical life.[21]

The Comedian never gets to experience this intimacy. Eddie first finds his clumsy attempts at making contact with his unacknowledged daughter, Laurie, rebuffed.[22] Then he cruelly rejects and shoots the Vietnamese woman who carries his unborn child.[23] Eddie comes to carry the scars of this last encounter to his final meeting with his daughter, which for Eddie turns out to be the most painful of all. This is the one moment in Eddie's life when he seems almost ready to let his mask slip—at a party held in his honor, when confronted by his now adult daughter Laurie.[24] The irony, for once, is getting to be too much even for Eddie Blake: he knows that this is a rotten crowd celebrating an even more rotten individual, all in the name of God and country. And in the middle of all this, he encounters the one thing in life he could legitimately be proud of, the woman Laurie has grown into. So he has to poke and to play with fire. "Kid, are you sure you wanna take this all the way?" he asks Laurie. *Kid.* He is trying to signal to Laurie who he really is, who she really is in relation to him; he is simultaneously trying to warn her off and invite her in.

And yet Eddie backs off from the brink. "Didn't take your old man's name, either," he hints darkly, but when Laurie asks what her name is to him, he lies: "Nothing." And when Laurie accuses him of forcing himself on her mother, all Eddie can do is reply feebly, "Only once."[25] This is as close to sincere as Eddie will ever get: he says one thing, means another, and because Laurie takes his words in yet a third way, the two never end up seeing eye to eye. The consequence is that when Laurie finally learns the truth, she can no longer deal with Eddie's paternity in terms other than to call it a "joke . . . big, stupid, meaningless."[26]

So it goes for Eddie Blake, all the way until the bitter end. Even when his Comedian's mask finally slips (quite literally—drunk and half-crazed, he goes around in full costume but without a mask) and he decides to level with somebody, he can only pour out his heart to a former enemy, Edgar Jacobi (aka Moloch), whom he knows will not understand and thus can be trusted with the information.[27] Eddie tells the truth, but only when he is safe in the knowledge that it will not be taken as such. "I guess it was his last performance," Moloch judges.[28] Is it, though? Eddie gets all emotional, demands to know the reasons why, prays to the mother of God—and does all of this in front of an audience that he knows will not have the slightest

clue about what is going on. What is performance and what is
real? Even Eddie doesn't know by the end. The hall of mirrors
has swallowed up the man, to the point where he could not get
out if he wanted to.[29]

Let's Put These Jokers through Some Changes

Kierkegaard never puts forward a general theory for what
prompts a move from one stage in life to another. Presumably,
some kind of paradigm shift is involved. In the case of the ironist,
what is needed is a shift from *aesthetics* to *ethics*, the "either"
and "or" referred to by Kierkegaard, and the passageway goes
through despair. Kierkegaard's aesthete lives for pleasant and
amusing experiences, for manipulating the world so that it will
reflect his whims and wishes. What Eddie needs to do is recognize that some things have value, over and above being merely
pleasant, or, conversely, that some deeds are simply wrong, no
matter how opportune they seem.

Perhaps Eddie has such an insight when he learns of Veidt's
monstrous plan. "I mean, I done some bad things," Eddie
confesses. "I did bad things to women. I shot kids! In 'Nam
I shot kids." But there comes a point where even the most
thickly laid-on irony will not cut it anymore: "I never did anything like, like . . . oh, Mother. Oh, forgive me."[30] In Moloch's
den—Moloch's mouth, the gates of hell!—Eddie finally gets
religion, or, rather, he is taken back to the ethical teachings he
presumably learned while growing up in a Catholic household,
teachings that suddenly and quite possibly for the first time
make sense to him.

Eddie's revelation occasions a meditation on Veidt's condition. Clearly, Veidt is both a monster and some kind of
superman, a madman and a genius, and ordinary people will
be hard-pressed to tell the difference.[31] He and Blake share a
disdain for ordinary people, while in other respects they stand

starkly opposed. Veidt describes the difference: "He sees me as an intellectual dilettante dabbling in national affairs that don't concern me. I see him as an amoral mercenary allying himself to whichever political faction seems likely to grant him the greatest license."[32] Yet in the end, Veidt himself is nothing but a glorified aesthete. All he wants to do is recreate the world in his own image, to establish a unity of thought and world on *his* terms, answerable to no one else—and certainly not to any moral code recognized by mere mortals. The gap between Veidt and the Comedian comes down to a mere difference in taste between order and chaos. Both are "intelligent men facing lunatic times."[33] It's just that Eddie Blake has given up on the notion of the world ever making sense, whereas Veidt still wishes to force his sense upon the world.

Neither Blake nor Veidt is able to recognize genuine duties toward other people who are viewed as equals in the way that, say, Dan Dreiberg does when he speaks of fraternity.[34] The latter would correspond to the ethical view of life, which for Kierkegaard consists in sincerely embracing generally held criteria for what is right and wrong, as well as attempting to lead one's life accordingly. The ethicist holds himself or herself accountable to communal standards of conduct, not out of a fear of punishment or in hopes of a reward but because that is the ethicist's existential *choice*. Out of the costumed adventurers, perhaps only the first Nite Owl would count as a do-gooder in the true sense, neither acting out a personal kink or power fantasy, nor striving to fulfill the wishes of others. (Hollis Mason's adventuring, after all, is merely an extension of his day job as a policeman.) Yet it is only through the ethical stage that one can proceed to what Kierkegaard regards as a higher form of questioning than irony, that is, humor in the proper sense of the word. In *Watchmen*, this is represented by the deadpan comedy of the vigilante Rorschach.

Never Surrender

Humor, according to Kierkegaard, mines a deeper vein of skepticism than irony does. Instead of any old finitude, the humorist's merriment evokes the notion of *sin*, which in turn presupposes a genuine moral sensibility.[35] A humorist is one who has lived an ethical life and has come to see its limitations, a person who has come face-to-face with the fundamentally flawed nature of human beings and who can now look on the gap between high ideal and low achievement with wry amusement. This results in the kind of situational humor that Rorschach deploys, one in which the tall orders of Big Figures (who are in fact small men) are dutifully pointed out and cut down to size.[36]

Compared with the ironist's endless head games, the humorist's brand of merriment is straightforward and revolves around a single truth: we all end up wading in the sewage, often head first.[37] But why doesn't the humorist simply let go of the ethical and retreat into a purely nihilistic position? At first glance, it seems as if Rorschach has indeed adopted a line of absolute self-creation and a repudiation of traditional values:

> Looked at sky through smoke heavy with human fat and God was not there. The cold, suffocating dark goes on forever, and we are alone. Live our lives, lacking anything better to do. Devise reason later. Born from oblivion; bear children, hellbound as ourselves; go into oblivion. There is nothing else. Existence is random. Has no pattern save what we imagine after staring at it for too long. No meaning save what we choose to impose.[38]

Yet there is a profound tension between this nihilistic version of Rorschach's story and one in which he continues to be driven by a moral purpose. In a previous meeting, Rorschach told his psychiatrist, Dr. Malcolm Long, "We do not do this thing because it is permitted. We do it because we have to. We do it because we are compelled."[39] And Rorschach stringently sticks to his perceived set of rules, having, for example, a propensity for acting in a bizarrely polite fashion at unexpected moments.[40] This, too, speaks against the notion of him having let go of the values he held before.

From the point of view of Kierkegaard's stages of life, Rorschach has embraced the notion of ethical responsibility, but without having recourse any longer to a belief in some karmic, cosmic balance (which would fit with the ethical life itself), or without having yet embraced a transcendent God who would straighten matters out (which would be the religious view). His bleak outlook on human nature looks deceptively like cynicism but is not. Instead, Rorschach's point is that if and when we go to hell in a handbasket (and hell itself is an ethical concept), we have only ourselves to blame. "This rudderless world is not shaped by vague metaphysical forces. It is not God who kills the children. Not fate that butchers them or destiny that feeds them to the dogs. It's us. Only us."[41]

A sense of humanity lingers in Rorschach's conduct: he can still feel sympathy in suffering and fellow-feeling in the face of certain death. These, too, mark out the good-humored in Kierkegaard's philosophy. When Rorschach hears that Moloch has terminal cancer, for instance, he gruffly spares the sick man.[42] Then, out of the blue, Rorschach acknowledges Dan's friendship.[43] Rorschach can still see himself in the eyes of a scared little boy and consequently let go of any grudges he may hold toward the mother.[44]

"Evil must be punished," Rorschach avers up until the end.[45] Veidt's actions are unacceptable because they are absolutely wrong, and his justifications only go to show that he remains below the ethical level. In fact, what does Rorschach say first on hearing of the others' willingness to compromise? "Joking, of course."[46] *Joking.* This is a joke that shouldn't be accepted for reality; there *is* still a meaningful distinction between reality and a madman's vision, even if no one else is willing to admit it.

Rorschach is right. There is something grotesque about the eagerness of Nite Owl, Silk Spectre, and Dr. Manhattan—all supposed "heroes"—to reach a conclusion that, let us not be coy, allows them to save their own skins while doing precisely nothing. Kierkegaard calls such people "armchair life-insurance salesmen," likening them to characters in ancient Roman comedies who brashly present themselves as fearless fighters, only to push others into the line of fire at the first sign of danger.[47] The effect is comic, Kierkegaard observes, and were Eddie Blake to be present, he would surely enjoy one final laugh at the so-called heroes' expense. The only way to bring "poetry" back onto the stage is to allow the lowly "sausage peddler" to rise to the occasion and show the audience what real heroism looks like. Does this remind anyone else of Rorschach?

Rorschach's resolution to stick with his chosen code of conduct parallels Dr. Long's and Detective Steve Fine's, both of whom are determined to break up the fight between Joey and her lover in chapter XI. "I'm still *me*," Fine snaps when a colleague suggests that he doesn't need to get to involved because of his suspension.[48] The ethical life is an internalized stance, not something that is done in order to satisfy some external set of expectations. Long, too, pleads with his wife in telling terms: "In a world like this . . . it's all we can do, try to help each other. It's all that means anything. . . . I can't run from it."[49] These are the determinations of fundamentally ethical human beings, for whom the recognition of absolute duty is the only thing that gives existence meaning.

Yet this also marks a distinction among Long, Fine, and Rorschach. The psychiatrist and the policeman both believe in the improvement of the human condition; they have to, if they are to perform their jobs properly. In Kierkegaard's eyes, the two are like married men who expect to be duly rewarded for their good conduct. But this is lacking in passion, for one thing, and so cannot occupy the highest level on the existential ladder: "in the period of courtship, to be absolutely certain that one is loved is a sure sign that one is not in love."[50] Rorschach's passion for justice, by contrast, comes without the expectation of the world reciprocating, and so reaches higher.

Never Look Down

Kierkegaard tells us that the great humorists are distinguished by their constant engagement with death. The limited length and precarious nature of all life gently mock even our best intentions and show up our noblest aims as falling far short of the mark. Rorschach shares this preoccupation with death, and yet he sticks to his perceived obligations: "Soon there will be war. Millions will burn. Millions will perish in sickness and misery. Why does one death matter against so many? Because there is good and there is evil, and evil must be punished. Even in the face of Armageddon I shall not compromise in this."[51]

We see a curious tension between an absolute commitment to duty and an absolute certainty that in the eyes of the world, it will all have been for naught. But what of the point of view of eternity? Kierkegaard tells us that we are in the presence of a true humorist when this question is answered "not with a yes or no of decision but with a sad smile."[52] Sure enough, when Rorschach is told by the hapless Dr. Long that there's hope, a tiny smile twinkles on Rorschach's lips.[53] Hope is not what the humorist deals in; it's how to cope with hopelessness that matters. How does Rorschach do it?

Rorschach's maxim "Just hang on by fingernails . . . and never look down"[54] resembles Kierkegaard's famous description of an existential *leap of faith*. It is precisely the move that puts the heart most at risk that lends it the deepest security. Naturally, at this point, "the slaves of the finite, the frogs in the swamp of life, scream: That kind of love is foolishness. . . .

Let them go on croaking in the swamp."[55] From the point of view of someone who has resolved to be faithful, despair is not only a mistake but a mortal sin.[56] There is a joyful abandonment that comes with the faithful person's recognition that his or her affections may well be spurned by this world and even go unrewarded in the next. Consider the following description from Kierkegaard as a summary of the differences between the Comedian and Rorschach:

> There is many a man who has been *immer lustig* [always merry] and yet stands so low that even esthetics regards him as comic. The question is whether one has not become joyful in the wrong place; and where is the right place? It is—in danger. To be joyful out on 70,000 fathoms of water, many, many miles from all human help—yes, that is something great! To swim in the shallows in the company of waders is not the religious.[57]

For all of his fancy moves, Blake is but a wader: due to his willingness to risk nothing (for even his own life to him means nothing), he stands to gain from all his efforts exactly that—nothing. By contrast, Rorschach's willfully blind commitment may seem both crazy and crazed, but it affords him a sense of satisfaction that will forever escape the Comedian. Herein lies another difference between the ironist and the humorist: because in his mind he has lived *for* something, Rorschach ends up with no regrets, while the Comedian, the negativity-fed sensualist, ends up with nothing but. As summed up by Rorschach, "For my own part, regret nothing. Have lived life, free from compromise . . . and step into the shadow now without complaint."[58]

For all this, Rorschach is not in Kierkegaard's religious stage, in which the singular becomes higher than the universal through a leap of faith. Instead of being such a *knight of faith*, Rorschach is a *knight of resignation*, precisely because he has given up all hope of a positive outcome to his passionately upheld beliefs and pursuits. A knight of faith would take heart in the promise of salvation arriving from the direction of the infinite, which is to say God, and so dare to embrace the ethical again. The knight of resignation cannot, because for him there simply is no God such as could effect a reconciliation between self and world. Thus the knight of resignation will find what comfort he can in his very hopelessness: "The knight . . . makes this impossibility possible by expressing it spiritually, but he expresses it spiritually by renouncing it."[59] For Kierkegaard, this ends up looking like a kind of weakness, an unwillingness to venture quite everything. The knight of resignation has shielded himself from further heartbreak by convincing himself that the matter has already been resolved; he has sown himself an iron shirt made out of tears.[60] The knight of faith would dare more.

It is significant that in the end, both the Comedian and Rorschach are reduced to tears.[61] They are stripped bare of every pretension to smug superiority; the masks are off, leaving them visible to us as Edward Morgan Blake and Walter Joseph Kovacs. The Comedian cries when the ethical stage of life suddenly dawns on him, while Rorschach is taken by surprise by his own inability to leave the ethical behind.

NOTES

1. *Watchmen*, chap. XI, p. 8.

2. From *Stages on Life's Way*, SV 6:443 = KW 11:476. SV refers to the first Danish edition of Kierkegaard's works, *Samlede Vaerker* (Copenhagen: Gyldendal, 1901–1906), while KW refers to the English trans. Howard and Edna Hong, in *Kierkegaard's Writings* (Princeton, NJ: Princeton University Press, 1978–2000).

3. *Concluding Unscientific Postscript*, SV 7:259 = KW 12/1:302.

4. See Sartre's *Being and Nothingness*, trans. Hazel Barnes (New York: Washington Square Press, 1992); on Kierkegaard and freedom, Arnold B. Come, *Kierkegaard as Humanist: Discovering My Self* (Montreal: McGill-Queen's University Press, 1995).

5. *Concluding Unscientific Postscript*, SV 7:304 = KW 12/1:351.

6. *Concluding Unscientific Postscript*, SV 7:88 = KW 12/1:109.

7. *Nicomachean Ethics*, Book i, chap. 8; compare Book ii, chap. 2.

8. *The Sickness unto Death*, SV 11:189–190 = KW 19:77–78.

9. *Watchmen*, chap. II, p. 18.

10. "Listen . . . once you figure out what a joke everything is, being the Comedian's the only thing makes sense." Ibid., p. 13.

11. Ibid., p. 10.

12. *Either/Or I*, SV 1:245 = KW 3:273.

13. See Andrew Cross, "Neither Either nor Or: The Perils of Reflexive Irony," in A. Hannay and G. D. Marino, eds., *The Cambridge Companion to Kierkegaard* (Cambridge, UK: Cambridge University Press, 1998), pp. 125–153.

14. *Watchmen*, chap. XI, p. 19.

15. Ibid., chap. II, p. 13.

16. Ibid., p. 9.

17. *The Concept of Irony*, SV 13:323–325 = KW 2:248–250.

18. *Watchmen*, chap. IX, p. 20.

19. Ibid., chap. XI, p. 18.

20. Ibid., chap. II, p. 3.

21. See, e.g., the essay by Kierkegaard's pseudonym "B" "The Esthetic Validity of Marriage" in *Either/Or II*, and the "Reflections on Marriage" contained in *Stages on Life's Way*.

22. *Watchmen*, chap. XI, pp. 15–16.

23. Ibid., chap. II, pp. 13–15.

24. Ibid., chap. IX, pp. 20–21.

25. Ibid.

26. Ibid., p. 26.

27. Ibid., chap. II, pp. 21–23; compare Veidt's comments in chap. XI, p. 25, and chap. XII, p. 20.

28. Ibid., chap. II, p. 21.

29. As Rorschach puts it, "No one else saw the joke. That's why he was lonely." Ibid., p. 27.

30. Ibid., p. 23.

31. As Nite Owl says, "How can anyone tell if he's gone crazy?" Ibid., chap. XI, p. 3.

32. Ibid., supplemental material, "After the Masquerade: Superstyle and the Art of Humanoid Watching," by Doug Roth, p. 10.

33. Ibid., p. 18.

34. Ibid., chap. VII, p. 28.

35. *The Concept of Irony*, SV 13:393 = KW 2:329.

36. *Watchmen*, chap. VIII, pp. 6–7.

37. Ibid., pp. 17–20.

38. Ibid., chap. VI, p. 26.

39. Ibid., p. 15.

40. For example, see ibid., chap. V, p. 6; chap. VIII, p. 21; and chap. X, p. 10.

41. Ibid., chap. VI, p. 26.

42. Ibid., chap. II, p. 24.

43. Ibid., chap. X, p. 10.

44. Ibid., p. 6.

45. Ibid., chap. XII, p. 23.

46. Ibid., p. 20.

47. *Stages on Life's Way*, SV 6:383–384 = KW 11:411–412.

48. *Watchmen*, chap. XI, p. 23.

49. Ibid., p. 20.

50. *Concluding Unscientific Postscript*, SV 7:396 = KW 12/1:455.

51. *Watchmen*, chap. I, p. 24.

52. *Concluding Unscientific Postscript*, SV 7:229 = KW 12/1:270.

53. *Watchmen*, chap. VI, p. 5.

54. Ibid., chap. X, p. 5.

55. *Fear and Trembling*, SV 3:92 = KW 6:41–42.

56. This point is extensively developed by Kierkegaard in *The Sickness unto Death*.

57. *Stages on Life's Way*, SV 6:437 = KW 11:470.

58. *Watchmen*, chap. X, p. 22.

59. *Fear and Trembling*, SV 3:94 = KW 6:44.

60. Ibid., SV 3:95–96 = KW 6:45.

61. *Watchmen*, chap. II, p. 23, and chap. XII, p. 24.

CONTRIBUTORS

Who Writes about the Watchmen?

Rob Arp is a research associate through the National Center for Biomedical Ontology at the University at Buffalo. He edited *South Park and Philosophy* (Blackwell, 2007) and coedited (with Mark D. White) *Batman and Philosophy* (Wiley, 2008). For Halloween, he dressed up as Rorschach—except he didn't need a mask.

James DiGiovanna is a substitute professor of philosophy at John Jay College of Criminal Justice/CUNY and a film critic for the *Tucson Weekly*. He has written on the aesthetics of fictional worlds, virtue theories of art and ethics, and issues of technology and identity. While working in the comics field, he once watched something terrifying crawl out of Alan Moore's beard, skitter across the floor, and become president of the United States.

Sarah K. Donovan is an assistant professor in the Department of Philosophy and Religious Studies at Wagner College in New York City. Her teaching and research interests include feminist, social, moral, and continental philosophy. Donovan feels lucky to have declined what seemed like a dream job offer after high school—to work as an apprentice for Adrian Veidt's creative team on a remote island in exchange for a free college education.

Christopher M. Drohan earned his PhD in the philosophy of media and communication in May 2007 from the European Graduate School in Switzerland. Currently, Drohan is the assistant director for the European Graduate School's Canadian Division and the chief editor of *Semiophagy: Journal of Pataphysics and Existential Semiotics*. Prior to his work at EGS, Drohan worked as a consultant for the infamous Veidt Corporation, until he was forced to flee the country because of racketeering charges.

Jacob M. Held's journal. February 10, 2009: I'm now an assistant professor of philosophy at the University of Central Arkansas. Areas of research: legal and political philosophy, nineteenth-century German philosophy, and applied ethics. Have written pieces on constitutional interpretation, gay marriage, euthanasia, and punishment. Coedited a decadent, self-indulgent volume of philosophical essays, *James Bond and Philosophy: Questions Are Forever*, and contributed to several other similar volumes. Write philosophy essays, lecture students, stare into the abyss of vacant eyes. There is nothing else. None of you philosophers understand, I'm not in this book with you, you're in this book with me.

J. Keeping is an assistant professor of philosophy at York University in Toronto, Canada. He has several publications in the journals *Philosophy Today* and *Phenomenology and the Cognitive Sciences* on topics that include emotions, instincts, cognition, and the philosophy of embodiment. In his alter ego as "J. F. Keeping," he also writes science fiction and fantasy and has recently been published in the magazine *Flashing Swords*! Professor Keeping enjoys wearing spandex and lurking on rooftops, but not at the same time.

Taneli Kukkonen is a research professor in antiquity at the University of Jyväskylä, Finland, having previously occupied the Canada Research Chair in the Aristotelian Tradition (Victoria, B.C.). He specializes in medieval cosmology and psychology and has published extensively on the Arabic reception of Aristotle and Plato. In *Battlestar Galactica and Philosophy* (Wiley, 2008), he indicated that polytheism is the way to go. He often feels like he doesn't quite get the jokes but laughs knowingly anyway.

J. Robert Loftis teaches at Lorain County Community College and writes occasionally on medical and environmental ethics. He wrote "Baltar the Tyrant?" for *Battlestar Galactica and Philosophy* (Wiley, 2008). Like Alan Moore, he worships a Roman snake god, but he only goes to temple on high holidays.

Aaron Meskin is a senior lecturer in philosophy at University of Leeds. Before moving to Leeds in 2005, he taught at Texas Tech University for six years. He has published articles in numerous journals and anthologies, on aesthetics, philosophical psychology, the philosophy of film, and the theory of information. He also serves as the aesthetics/philosophy-of-art editor for the online journal *Philosophy Compass*, and he recently coedited *Aesthetics: A Comprehensive Anthology* (Wiley-Blackwell, 2007). Meskin's most valued possession is a complete set of the first thirty issues of *Tales of the Black Freighter* in mint condition.

Alex Nuttall is currently researching quality TV shows, excellent movies, and engaging video games. He received an MA in philosophy from Purdue University and enjoys studying ethics and aesthetics. He is seeking to join the ethics board at the Institute of Extraspacial Studies.

Nicholas Richardson is an associate professor in the Department of Physical Sciences at Wagner College in New York City, where he teaches general, advanced inorganic, and medicinal chemistry. He may have worked with Dr. Manhattan at the Rockefeller Military Research Center, but he's sworn to secrecy about those times.

Christopher Robichaud is an instructor in public policy at the Harvard Kennedy School of Government. Robichaud and his colleague Professor Milton Glass believe they were working on the definitive academic analysis of Dr. Manhattan; however, the manuscript no longer exists—anywhere—and the memories of writing it are murky at best. It's as if some superpowerful being decided—oh, wait a minute . . .

Tony Spanakos—since passage of the Keene Act—has gone underground as an assistant professor of political science and law at Montclair State University and an adjunct assistant professor of politics at New York University. He has written articles and book chapters about political economy, democracy, and violence in Latin America and coedited the book *Reforming Brazil* (Rowman & Littlefield, 2004). He has been a Fulbright Visiting Professor in Brazil (2002) and Venezuela (2008), where he helped hunt Latin America's supervillains while a member of Super-Menudo. Spanakos narrowly lost out on his bid on eBay for Rorschach's journal. (Damn you, Kevin Federline, for your surprisingly savvy pop culture sensibilities!)

Andrew Terjesen is currently a visiting assistant professor of philosophy at Rhodes College in Memphis, Tennessee. In the past, he has taught at Washington and Lee University, Austin College, and Duke University. He is mainly interested in ethics, moral psychology, early modern philosophy, and the philosophy of economics. He has had essays published in this series on the connections between philosophy and *Family*

Guy, *The Office*, and *Battlestar Galactica* and is preparing essays involving *Heroes* and the X-Men. Terjesen would like to separate himself into multiple iridescent blue bodies so that he could juggle everything but hesitates for fear that it would creep out his wife, too.

Arthur Ward is a PhD student in the department of philosophy at Bowling Green State University. His main areas of interest are metaethics, applied ethics, and the philosophy of biology. He is currently writing his dissertation on the concept of *fittingness* and its application in the arenas of justice, virtue, and value. Forgetful when caught up in his research, he has been known to occasionally leave his intrinsic field at the office by mistake.

Mark D. White is an associate professor in the Department of Political Science, Economics, and Philosophy at the College of Staten Island/CUNY, where he teaches courses that combine economics, philosophy, and law. He has edited (with Robert Arp) *Batman and Philosophy* (Wiley, 2008), *Theoretical Foundations of Law and Economics* (Cambridge, 2009), and, with Barbara Montero, *Economics and the Mind* (Routledge, 2007). He has also written dozens of scholarly articles and book chapters, plus philosophical essays on Metallica, *South Park*, *Family Guy*, *The Office*, and the X-Men. But his greatest claim to fame is beating Adrian Veidt at Risk (once).

INDEX

After the Masquerade